Beyond Petty

Embracing Dreams
Defying the Odds

Ricky L. Petty, Sr.

I

Published by
Protective Hands Communications
Riviera Beach, FL 33404
Phone: 561-440-4144
Website: www.protectivehands.com
Email: info@protectivehands.com

Printed in the United States of America

Contents

Acknowledgements

Achieving success is a team effort. It's impossible to get far without a solid support system surrounding you. Without a doubt, I owe a huge thanks to a host of people, organizations, and institutions that have played a crucial part in my life and helped me along my journey. Topping the list is God, who deserves all the glory for the blessings in my life.

My family has been my rock. A big shoutout to my beautiful mother, Annie Petty, Aunt Carolyn Petty, my amazing children Ricky Petty Jr., Rickia Petty, and Rickiya Petty, my sisters Latasha Petty, Carla Brown and Fiero Brown, my brother Tony Cobb, and all my cousins and great Aunts. I also remember my late Grandmother Laura Ann Petty and Uncle Benjamin Burton Jr. with love.

Life threw its fair share of curveballs my way, but I managed to navigate through them, thanks to my prayer warriors which include my church families at Greater St. Paul AME and St. John Missionary Baptist Church. I owe a special thanks to Rev. Dr. Lee Harvin Sapp, Pastor Quincy Cohen, Pastor Nathaniel Robinson III, Pastor Richard Rathel, Pastor Richard Dames, Pastor Rae Whitely, Vontell Mills, Kemberly Bush, Rita Simmons, Katherine Burns, and many others who've kept me in their prayers.

I'm deeply inspired by the words of Dr. Mary McLeod Bethune: *"Enter to Learn and Depart to Serve,"* and I'm eternally grateful for the doors opened for me at Bethune Cookman University. That institution and its people mean the world to me.

A huge thank you to my Omega Psi Phi Fraternity Inc. brothers. Joining the organization was one of the best decisions of my life. I have been enriched with lifelong friendships and invaluable lessons.

Thanks to the organizations that took a chance on me:

Workforce Alliance, Children Home's Society, Palm Health Foundation, and Pathways to Prosperity. Each opportunity allowed me to serve, learn, grow, and earn a living.

I can't forget my hometown, Boynton Beach, Florida. The love and support from this community has been amazing.

To everyone that has supported me and my business over the years and contributed to my success; educators, friends, business partners and clients, I would like to say thank you.

To the mothers of my amazing children, thank you for being the women that you are and caring for our children. Without your support, my journey would've been nearly impossible.

To Shalena Taylor, my ride or die. Your unwavering love and support has been a light in some of my darkest moments. Thank you for who you are and what you've been in my life.

With great blessings come great responsibility. I'm committed to giving back and I'm motivated by the incredible support I've received. Here's to continuing the journey, inspired by God's grace and the support of those around me.

Introduction

Hey there, I'm Ricky Petty, and I want to extend a warm welcome to you as we dive into the pages of my life. Now, you may be wondering what this book is about and what's in it for you. Well, stick around, because you're in for a ride, a journey through the highs, the lows, and everything in between.

See, I'm a middle-aged Black man who's lived through the kind of stories you've probably only seen in the movies or heard about in the news. But I'm not here to simply tell you my story; I'm here to share the lessons, the wisdom, and yeah, the gems that I've picked up along the way. From the streets of South Florida to the boardrooms of successful businesses, I've seen it all.

I grew up in a world where stability was a luxury, and life was anything but predictable. But the streets and their challenges taught me something valuable. They taught me how to survive, how to thrive, and most importantly, how to transform adversity into opportunity.

In these pages, you're gonna find real talk. I'm gonna share with you the good, the bad, and the ugly. We're gonna laugh together, we might even shed a tear or two, but most of all, we're going to learn. Learn about life, about resilience, and about the power of never giving up.

You see, this book isn't just my story, it's a roadmap. A roadmap that I hope will help guide you through your own journey, helping you navigate your own challenges, and inspiring you to reach for your own version of success.

So, you can expect raw, unfiltered stories from the heart. You can expect lessons on how to turn lemons into lemonade, and insights on how to elevate your life, no matter where you're starting from. Hopefully, you'll gain a new perspective on life, and find the strength to break free from whatever chains are holding you back.

We're gonna talk family, community, hustle, and the relentless pursuit of greatness. We're gonna explore what it means to be Black in America. The unique challenges we face, and how to turn those challenges into steppingstones towards success.

So, buckle up because this journey, it's about to get real. And who knows? By the end of this book, you might just find yourself ready to take on the world, armed with a new set of tools, a fresh perspective, and the knowledge that no matter where you come from, greatness is within your reach.

Much love and respect,

Ricky L. Petty, Sr.

PART ONE
The Formative Years

Chapter One
Humble Beginnings

"I was born into a world that had already counted me out."

Born on January 24, 1979, in Spartanburg, South Carolina, I was a child of possibility, wrapped in adversity. I remember being a kid in the Phillis Goins Projects, putting on my Michael Jackson jacket and strutting my shit down the sidewalk like I was on stage, moonwalking my little ass off, and the crowd went wild. The neighbors were my audience, applauding, hollering, and cheering. Even then, I was entertaining folks, and damn, it felt good!

Picture this, if you can. An old stretch of well-worn brick, nestled right in the heart of Spartanburg, South Carolina. We're talking '80s here and my recollections seem to be draped in this old-timey sepia shade. That's where my roots got their start, deep in the fertile earth of the projects. I was just a jitterbug when Mama decided it was time we hit the road to South Florida.

Now, the projects ain't always a pretty sight to behold. Scuffed and scarred by years of hard living, they stood like solemn sentinels to the struggles and dreams of the folks who called them home. My folks, we were poor, at least if you measured wealth in the dollars and cents way. But if you took a closer look, you'd find a kind of richness that Wall Street could never dream of quantifying. We didn't have much of anything, but we had us and that was plenty. Our homes were close-knit, and not only because we were packed in tight like sardines in a can. We were woven together, stitched up by the shared struggles and the shared laughter, the shared pain, and the shared joy. No, the fabric of our lives wasn't silk or velvet, it was raw denim, tough, resilient, and full of character.

My maternal Grandma, Laura Petty, was a force of nature or so I'm told. She was the fifth child of eight children: six sisters and one brother. A resilient matriarch, she and two of her sisters, my great aunts, traded the familiarity of their old stomping grounds for the promise of a fresh start in the Sunshine State back in the '60s. They packed up their hopes and dreams, embarking on a journey to South Florida, seeking the warmth of its sun, and the balm of its ocean breezes. But you see, life, it's got a funny way of twisting hopes into trials.

I never got the chance to meet my Grandma Laura. Before I could even register her face, her voice, and her laughter, she was ripped away from our family. The place was Delray Beach, Florida, the year was 1975, the year that stamped a permanent mark of sorrow on our family tapestry.

So, it's only through stories passed down that I've known Grandma Laura. The stories painted her as a woman of grit and grace. Yet, the stories couldn't fill the void her sudden death left.

The details are fuzzy, but the harsh reality is very clear. The man we knew as Granddaddy Ben, my Uncle Ben and Aunt Hattie's father, he was at the center of it. The irony?

This man was family, bound to us by blood and name. But with a single bullet, a deadly dance of fate, and grandma was no more, her life snuffed out in the blink of an eye.

The incident was shrouded in a haze of confusion and disbelief. It was too much to take in, too hard to swallow. The authorities called it an accident. A stray bullet that found its mark. A fatal mishap. But to us, it was more than just an accident. It was a devastating storm that shifted our family tree. It's a story etched deep into our family narrative, a tale of loss and pain, of unanswered questions.

Grandma Laura's absence is a wound that has never quite healed, a gap that never got bridged. It's a scar we carry, a part of our history we can never erase, no matter how much the Florida sun shines on us.

I was born into a world that had already counted me out. See, back in the early 1980s, a young Black man like myself was expected to be just another statistic. In 1980, studies show that only 38% of Black teen mothers managed to finish high school, compared to a solid 50% of their white counterparts. It's a harsh reality, but the truth cuts deep.

My mama wasn't in that 38%, so life for her and by extension, for me, was going to be an uphill battle, no doubt about it. Her lack of a high school diploma meant low paying jobs with long hours or no job at all. It was a whole lot of struggle.

Higher education? That was a rare privilege. A meager 6% of Black teen moms made it past high school, compared to a good 25% of white teen moms. It was more than just an uphill battle; it was scaling a cliff with your bare hands.

Now, the percentage of teen mothers who were Black had been on a steady rise, jumping from 7% in 1970 to 12% by the start of the 80s. As for the poverty rate, well, those numbers were grim. In 1980, a staggering 83% of single Black teen mothers were living below the poverty line, more than double the national average of 40%. The figures might've improved slightly towards the end of the decade, but they were far from what you'd call encouraging.

Education, they say, is the key to unlocking doors, but without it, my mama found herself facing locked doors and dead ends. Despite this, she was determined, relentless, and downright stubborn in her fight to provide for us, carving out a life from what little she had. Her strength wasn't written in diplomas or degrees, but in the unwavering resolve that shone in her eyes, a testament to her will to beat the odds.

Life threw me into this battleground, armed me with hope, and told me to survive, so that's what I did. I was determined not to be another number in a grim statistic. I was gonna carve my own path. My father was absent from the picture, leaving my mother to raise me.

Let me paint a picture for y'all about growing up. You know how kids are always eager to brag about their folks? Well, my crew and I, we'd sit around, just chatting away, each one trying to one-up the other. "My daddy this," one would say. "My daddy that," another would chime in.

Now, I never really knew my dad like that, but I wanted to fit in, feel included. So, one day, I piped up with, "Well, my daddy's a lawyer!" I thought I nailed it, right? But man, my mama overheard me. She yelled loudly for everyone to hear.

"Boy, your daddy ain't shit! Your daddy smoke rocks." And I was like, "Well dang, Ma!" Talk about getting put on blast! But that's life, isn't it? Always keeps you humble, always keeps you grounded.

As I said, we were born in a place far from Florida, but eventually, my family decided to move there in the hopes of creating a better life for all of us.

I am the oldest of three children with a five-year age gap between us. My brother Tony was born after we had been in Florida for some time. Despite the struggles we faced, my mother worked tirelessly to ensure that we had everything we needed.

I remember the Greyhound bus ride like it was yesterday, but in fact it was 1984. Me, my mother, and my sister Tasha, we were all packed up and ready for a new beginning. We had a bag with two pork chop sandwiches and three sodas, our only sustenance for the journey. It wasn't much, but it was enough to keep us going.

We rolled into Boynton Beach, Florida, and found ourselves under the same roof as Granddaddy Ben and a sweet lady we knew as Grandma Ruth. This woman, she held a special place in the heart of Granddaddy Ben. Yeah, the same man who, in a tragic twist of fate, was behind the accidental death of my Grandma Laura. It was a complicated weave of relationships, a bitter-sweet blend of new beginnings and painful histories.

We stayed with them for a few months, settling in as best we could. I attended Rolling Green Elementary, walking to school alongside my Uncle Ben. He was in the sixth grade, while I was just a kindergartener trying to find my way.

I can still picture it clear as day, Aunt Granny and her crew rolling down to Florida just a handful of months after we got settled. Aunt Granny, she was my mama's sister, a spitfire if there ever was one. She brought a whole posse of my cousins with her: Dank, Seaweed, Nannyboo, and Stuffy. Their names alone echoed of our Carolina roots, a slice of home they brought along with them.

I remember that day like it was yesterday, their wide-eyed expressions as they took in their new home in sunny South Florida. Before they could even get comfortable, I laid down the law. I let 'em know in no uncertain terms that those old South Carolina nicknames they loved to tease me with, 'Fe Fe', 'Pudding', 'Shynana', had no place in this new chapter. I was Ricky here, and if they strayed away from the script, they would catch these hands. They knew I meant business and quickly fell in line, dropping those old nicknames and sticking to calling me Ricky.

Life took us to Delray Beach next, which is right next door to Boynton. There we bunked up with Aunt Jolly and Aunt Bay, our great aunts, and grandma's sisters. New city, new place to live, new school.

I was just a first grader when I first set foot in Delray Beach Elementary, carrying all the jitters of a newbie. Starting at a new school ain't no walk in the park, there's always some kind of challenge lurking around the corner. For me, the first one came in the form of a kickball game.

Back in the day, man, I was like the Michael Jordan of kickball. I could kick that ball to kingdom come and back. No joke. Every time I stepped up to the plate, the outfielders would back up, bracing themselves for the rocket I was about to launch. They knew when Ricky was up, that ball was going deep!

So, there I was one day, poised and ready. The anticipation was high, the fielders stepping back in respect. I bolted towards the ball, swung my leg, and WHAM! The ball went sailing... but so did my shoe.

Mama had bought me these cheap *Easy Walkers* from the corner store, which probably set her back all of $3.99. They were size nines, and I was a size 6. I had to stuff 'em with toilet paper just so they'd stay on my feet. When I sent that ball skyward, my shoe launched off, and a storm of toilet paper followed. It was like a damn ticker-tape parade, only less celebratory.

The field erupted in laughter, their laughs echoing through my humiliation. As I scrambled to gather my shoe and the snowy trail of toilet paper it left behind, I could feel the heat of embarrassment flooding my cheeks. Man, I was more embarrassed than a cat caught climbing out the wrong tree. Yeah, it was one hell of a day, seared into my memory forever.

There was this other time, though, that stands out, even today. This was the roughest of the rough. Time was ticking toward the 2 o'clock bell, freedom almost within grasp. I was desperate, you know. I remember turning to my teacher, her stern face staring down at me, pleading to be excused to the restroom. She wasn't having none of it, though. I asked again, and again. But the thing about nature is, when it calls, it ain't really asking for permission.

It happened right there, in the middle of that sunlit classroom. The sensation of it running down my legs still makes me cringe, but what cut deeper was the laughter. My heart sank and I could almost hear it echoing in my chest. This pretty girl, who I was crushing on, just up and says, "What's that smell? Smells like doo doo."

Soon enough, the whole classroom was rolling with laughter, while I stood there, feeling smaller than a roach under a boot. I was stuck, man. Lower than low. My teacher, as stern as she was, she wasn't without mercy. She led me to the office, gave me a chance to clean up. Swapping my stained clothes for something cleaner felt like a small victory amidst a losing battle. Sitting there, waiting for my mom to come get me, I could still hear the ghosts of their laughter.

When we packed up and moved back to Boynton Beach, I enrolled in Poinciana Elementary School, and I couldn't have been happier. I was leaving behind the stinging shame of those moments, thankful that I wouldn't have to look those faces in the eye again.

You see, we all got our struggles, our tests. They're nothing but steppingstones, though. They help us grow; they shape us. And me? Oh, I sure did grow. Came up strong, learned from every stumble, every fall. Nothing can hold me down for long, you know what I mean?

Yet, every bit of sunlight casts a shadow, and my story wasn't always bathed in the golden Florida sun. As I grew, the world around me shifted, twisted into a darker reality. As a sun-soaked child of the South Florida streets, raised by the strength of a single young mother, I lived a tale darker than the night skies. My existence was spun from a mosaic of poverty, struggle, and resilience. It was a tableau colored by the stark realities of the crack epidemic that stormed our neighborhoods in the '80s.

See, my mama and her sister, they fell victim to that hellish cooked up powder. The crazy thing is their Auntie introduced them to it. Like many others, they were trapped in its grip, a death grip that swallowed lives and dreams whole, reducing vibrant souls to hollow shells.

During the day, the sun shined brightly, casting golden hues across our vibrant neighborhoods. But come nightfall, those same streets were choked by the unseen hands of the epidemic. It was a monster, ruthless and unforgiving. It didn't discriminate. It swallowed up our mothers, our fathers, our brothers, and sisters. This sinister presence hovered over us; a lurking specter ready to snatch the joy out of our lives.

Our tight-knit Black communities, once overflowing with life, became the epicenter of a crack epidemic. Strong, proud men were turned into mere whispers of their former selves. Mothers struggled against the yoke of addiction, and innocent children, like me, were forced to grow up too soon.

I watched the crack epidemic ravage Black families, stripping them of their dignity, unity, and hope. Fathers became phantoms, mothers transformed into martyrs, and children? We were the collateral damage of a war we never asked for. Soldiers in a war we never enlisted for. The epidemic was more than just a drug problem. It was a social earthquake, fracturing the very bedrock of our communities.

The aftershocks are still felt today, decades later. The generation born into the epidemic has grown up now, many of us still bearing the deep scars of our past. We carry with us a story of resilience and survival, a story that must be told, remembered, and learned from.

And so, we press on, our memories are like the old slave spirituals. We have songs of sorrow but also of hope, resilience, and resistance. We remember our mothers, our sisters, and all the others taken too soon, not as victims, but as fighters. We remember them and honor their strength as we keep their stories alive, transforming the narrative of Black communities from victims to victors.

In the face of a brutal storm, we stood, we fell, but we rose again, learning to dance even in the rain. That's the story of South Florida's Black communities and of many Black communities across America. A tale of trials and triumphs, of love and loss, and ultimately, of survival.

My mother was more than just a statistic. She was more than just another Black woman swallowed by the crack epidemic. She was a survivor, like so many mothers in our community, but with battle scars. Her eyes carried stories of struggle, but also a fierce determination. She fought. Oh, how she fought.

The year 1990, that was a game-changer for Mama. The year before, she had managed to escape a relationship, the kind that left more scars on the inside than on the out. She managed to break free from the iron grip of that damned crack, though she still danced with alcohol. The final push, the catalyst that sprung Mama into action, came on the heels of a tragedy.

1990 was the year we lost my little brother, Chucky to SIDS, the silent thief known as *Sudden Infant Death Syndrome.* But through the shroud of grief and loss, Mama found an ember of resilience. That's right, Mama was more than just a survivor. She was a warrior, a beacon of tenacity in the face of adversity.

Mama took a job cleaning hotels, a job that may not sound like much, but it kept us fed. Every day she'd go in, her spirit strong, her determination unwavering. There she was, scrubbing down rooms, changing sheets, all to put some food on our table. That was Mama. She was a tower of strength, strong spirit. We weren't exactly living the high life, but we were managing. Had a bit more stability, a taste of independence. It wasn't riches, but it was progress. We were slowly crawling our way out of the hole, one day, one cleaned hotel room at a time.

And that's how my humble beginnings shaped me, pushing me to strive for a brighter future despite all the challenges that lay ahead. It was just the beginning of my journey, but I was determined to rise above it all. It's a tale of strength, of determination, of transcending boundaries.

I am Ricky L. Petty, Sr., a boy born into the raw, real charm of Spartanburg, South Carolina to a survivor of the rough streets of South Florida. A young man standing tall in the face of life's trials, and a testament to the fact that no matter where you start, it's where you're headed that matters.

This is my story, and I've just turned the first page. The journey is long, the road winding, but I'm ready to move beyond petty and make my mark.

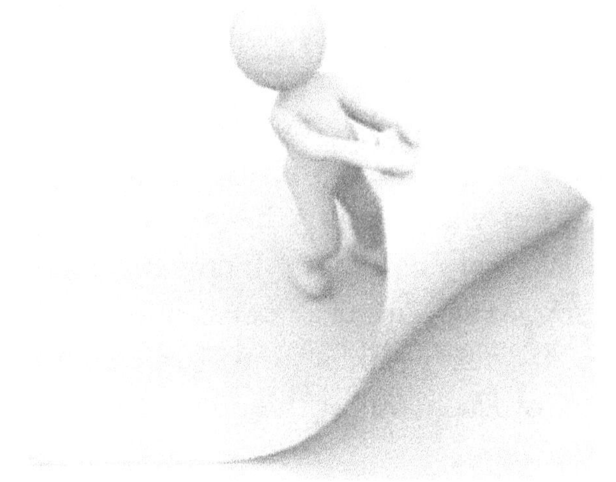

Chapter Two
The Sting of Poverty

"Even when life gives you a tough hand, you can still play a good game."

The weight of an empty pocket is something I became familiar with early on. I remember days when the pangs of hunger seemed to strike a chord with the groans of old floorboards in our home. I remember nights when the cold seemed to seep right through the walls, chilling our bones.

In this chapter, I want to take you on a walk through the streets of my past—a place where dreams sometimes seemed distant and out of reach, but the spirit of hope never faded.

Poverty wasn't just a lack of material wealth for me; it was an environment, an ever-present background hum that colored every experience. But let me tell you, as oppressive as it was, poverty was also a masterful teacher. It taught me the value of grit, the art of hustle, and the true meaning of community. The shadows cast by empty refrigerators and worn-out shoes threw into sharp relief the warmth of shared meals, the joy of hand-me-down stories, and the unyielding strength of family ties.

Allow me to share with you the bitter taste of want, but more importantly, the fire it kindled within me. The urge to not just survive, but to thrive. To not only dream, but to chase those dreams with an unyielding intensity. As you journey through these pages with me, I hope you see that while poverty left its mark, it was but a chapter in a greater narrative—a narrative of resilience, growth, and undying hope. Let's take this journey together.

Back in the day, the value of a dollar was a lesson learned early on. Scratch and scrape was the name of the game, for lack was the only rhythm we danced to. It was a tough hand to be dealt, but it honed a certain hustle spirit, a drive to push through those trying circumstances.

The world we grew up in was a tight-knit community of blood and chosen family. Mama, her dude, my sister, Auntie, her dude, my cousins, and I were all holed up together in our little one-bedroom house.

Twelve people under one roof at times may seem like a crowd to some, but it was home to us. Eating out was a luxury we couldn't afford, but Auntie, bless her soul, had a magic touch in the kitchen. I can still taste those heartwarming breakfasts of grits, eggs, and sizzling bologna, which would curl up like a smile on a griddle. When the bologna bubbled up in the center, you just knew it was going to be good! Less than four bucks, that's all it took to fill us all up.

Back-to-school shopping was a minimalist event, definitely not like it is for some kids today. Mama would get me two pairs of shorts, one pair of jeans, three shirts, and a pair of XJ900s. I bet some of y'all don't even know what a XJ900 is. Well, I can tell you they were not Air Jordans, and they only cost about $11.99. Barely $60 spent for everything, but I was set for the school year.

Our modes of transportation were limited, driver's licenses and cars were luxuries we couldn't afford. Instead, we relied on city buses and kind neighbors to get us where we needed to be.

We didn't have much and it forced us to go out and get it. I started my hustle young and so did my cousins. We would go fishing in the canal and sell the fish to our next-door neighbors. We really started making good money when we began selling mangoes and oranges to folks in the neighborhood, learning the skills of negotiation, customer service, and building up our customer base while still in knee pants. My cousins and I knew where to find the ripest fruit, and when school was out, we were up at the break of dawn filling our buckets.

I was always down to make some money, I even had my own candy shop set up right in school, raking in a pretty penny. By the fourth grade, I was buying my own sneakers, trading up those XJ900s for a sleek pair of navy-blue Converses. I felt like I was stepping up in the world!

But poverty cast long shadows on my early education and social interactions. Our world was limited by a lack of resources and knowledge. My world was school, and that was it. There were no extracurricular activities, no summer camps, no family vacations. Field trips and school activities were luxuries we often couldn't afford. When I began to play baseball, I remember having to make do with a righthanded baseball glove even though I was a lefty.

My wardrobe was often the target of schoolyard jokes, but I learned to deflect with humor. When resources are sparse, priorities shift—survival tops the list, education and health take a backseat.

The poverty of my upbringing had a profound impact on my ambitions and dreams. My world was one of limited opportunities, of low-quality education and scarce healthcare. But my world was also one filled with a sense of hopelessness, a belief that dreams were unattainable. I had to grow up quickly, responsibilities thrust upon me at an age when most kids were still playing with toys.

I began to see my poverty not as a curse, but as a catalyst. Yes, it was a difficult life. Yes, it limited my opportunities and resources, but it also sparked a fierce ambition and an unwavering determination within me. It made me realize that if you want to change your circumstances, you must be the catalyst for that change. So, I hustled. I sold fish, I sold fruit and candy, I cleaned yards, I sold newspaper subscriptions, and I gambled. From the age of nine, I was a businessman in my own right. And I was proud of it.

Yeah, that's how we lived. That's how we grew up. It was tough as hell, but damn, it was life. It was real. And it was ours. At times when I had extra money, I would lend to family members and earn interest on the borrowed amount. It was all part of the hustle. The losses were hard when they defaulted, but it only drove me to hustle harder. The lack of certain luxuries in life will force you to become innovators and that is something no one could take from us.

We created opportunities out of thin air. I remember those days when my cousins and I would scout for mango and orange trees, picking ripe fruit and filling up buckets. Then we'd take to the streets, selling our fruit and bringing in the dollars. Struggles have a way of teaching you the art of the hustle.

Those little fruit sales earned us a couple of bucks here and there, enough to get us candy, snacks, marbles, or even a couple rounds of video games at the corner store. We could also visit the candy lady, trading coins for Lilly Dillies, pickled eggs, cookies, and cakes. And then there was the ice cream truck. When we were short on cash, we'd claim it was our birthday. Got us free bubble gum every time. Funny thing is, I seemed to have a birthday three times a month.

Poverty was a tough teacher, but it taught me one thing above all: success isn't served on a silver platter, you've got to hustle for it. Growing up with less instilled in me a fierce ambition, and an appreciation for the value of hard work and creativity. No matter how bleak the circumstances, I knew I had the power to change my story.

Stability was a concept as foreign as caviar on a McDonald's menu, a luxury we couldn't afford to taste. Just as Florida's weather can shift from sunshine to storm in a heartbeat, our living situations morphed at a similar pace. As frequently as one might change a radio station, our addresses were in a state of flux, each a new stanza in our ever-evolving urban ballad.

Each spin of the calendar delivered a fresh landscape – new walls offering a different slice of the world presented through our window, and a continually refreshed register of neighbors. All our homes were within shouting distance of each other, crowded into a few condensed city blocks.

The idea of dialing up a moving company was like dreaming of having a spaceship. A car? Huh, that was a privilege that our poverty-stricken existence couldn't unlock. Neither Mama nor Auntie had ever wrestled with a steering wheel or pressed down on an accelerator during those days. Our reality didn't stretch that far. So how did we orchestrate these moves, these geographical relocations, without a vehicle or the coin to secure a mover's assistance? We huddled and did what folks in our circumstances do. We clenched our teeth, flexed our muscles, and shouldered every piece of our lives to the new location ourselves.

There's something that checks your pride, but also oddly empowering, about hauling your entire life down the block. I mean literally walking with our arms loaded with mattresses, couches, dressers—the whole nine yards of what we owned. It was a humbling experience, casting a harsh light on our struggle. I can't front, there were moments when our makeshift parade turned into a spectacle, filling me with a kind of shame. But with time, you grow skin thick enough to shield you from those prying eyes, from the whispered judgments.

Yet, the fascinating part was the promise of a fresh start. The allure of uncharted territory often overshadowed the shame. Each strenuous move, no matter how backbreaking, was brushed with a sense of anticipation. We were venturing into a new home, just a notch better than the previous, but fresh, nonetheless. From the numbered Avenues - 12th, 11th, 10th, to the historic MLK Jr. Boulevard, then on to 13th Ave, 4th St., Cherry Hill, and finally landing in the Projects.

Our life journey was an elaborate maze mapped within the heart of Boynton Beach. Over fifteen moves, each one a steppingstone etching the path of our lives. We were getting by, just about, but one thing held true, we knew how to mine joy from the most ordinary of things. We were kids of the streets and the soil. We found pleasure in marbles, worn-out mattresses, and the fresh fruit the seasons gave us.

Being nestled in the house, battling the hardships that came packaged with it, the experience was nothing short of a rollercoaster. The days when my mom and Auntie would get into some heated exchanges, over a disagreement, it felt like living in a house split in two. That was the daily grind, the routine we fell into, navigating those volatile waters.

But there was a positive aspect. Me and my cousins, we grew up close-knit, as tight as most siblings. Even though our blood said cousins, our bond spelled brothers and sisters. In a world where resources were scarce, we learned the art of sharing, of dividing our limited possessions without the bitterness of want. Holidays became a beacon of unity amidst the struggle. Even in our struggles, there was joy to be found, moments of levity that pierced the gloom.

Halloween, for instance, was a different beast altogether. No fancy costumes or high-priced masks for us. Instead, we had two options: a white sheet and a face full of flour or the use of Mama's make-up and you'd be a clown. That was our go-to look, our staple. A homegrown attempt to fit into the season. Still, despite the simplicity, it stirred up a cocktail of laughter and excitement, producing moments we relished.

As for the trick-or-treating, forget the glossy, colorful bags that screamed commercialism. We had our trusty pillowcases, a Winn Dixie Supermarket bag, maybe. Either one was practical and roomy enough to hold the night's loot.

We'd set off, eager as a pack of wolves, ready to hit house after house. By the end of the night, those bags would be brimming with candy, a testimony to our fruitful expedition. Those were the good times, the memories that stitched patches of joy into our humble upbringing.

Back in the day, we didn't always have access to the fancy name-brand stuff. There were Christmases when our wish lists had to take a back seat to reality. Although I believed in

Santa Claus, I was starting to question his fairness or me being undeserving because there was this one wish that I consistently harbored, like a glowing ember in my heart. I wanted Santa Claus to bring me a remote-control car with batteries and no string. Each year, he would deliver on half of that wish, a shiny new remote-controlled car. Yet, there was always a missing piece – the batteries and the car had a string.

So, my cousin and I would engage in a race of imagination, pushing our lifeless toy cars, while taunting each other. "Just wait til I get my batteries, my car will leave yours in the dust." But fate had a twisted sense of humor. By the time we managed to lay our hands on those elusive batteries, our cars would be in such a state of disrepair that the dream of a high-speed chase was nothing more than just that, a sweet dream.

Year after year, my Christmas wish remained unchanged, a remote-controlled car, no fancy frills needed, and most importantly, a set of batteries and NO string! Eventually, I realized there was no Santa Claus, and it was Mama who managed to score the package, the car. But she did so just a day before Christmas, leaving us no time to buy the batteries. So close, yet so far, our anticipations deflated once more.

I recall this one time when I was around six years old, Mama bought me a Big Wheel. Now, you'd think a boy of six would have graduated to a bicycle, and you'd be right. I knew I was older than most kids riding Big Wheels but that didn't quell the joy I felt riding it. Sure, it was a Big Wheel, not a bicycle, but it was my Big Wheel, a symbol of my mother's struggle and her love for me. I was proud of that Big Wheel, proud of where I came from, and proud of the resilience we harbored.

We didn't need fancy toys or expensive gizmos. Nah, all we needed was a discarded mattress sitting on a trash pile. That rundown piece of bedding was our playground. Every day, the neighborhood kids, a motley crew of scrappy souls, would gather 'round that mattress. We'd jump, we'd flip, wrestle, even throw down and fight if need be. Hours would slip by like minutes, the echo of our laughter punctuating the air.

And then there was the marble game, as much a part of our childhood as the Florida sun. A bag of marbles would set you back about a dollar, give or take, depending on the fancy level of your glassy treasures. But all you really needed was a handful of good ones, four or five maybe, and you were in the game.

We roamed around on foot or bikes, hunting down the best marble arenas. The air was always thick with the excitement of the game, phrases like "Loud as a church bell!" "Rounders no rounders back!" "No nothing for you through the whole game" became our battle cries.

But, it was more than just a game, it was a life class in disguise. It taught us about friendships, about trust, about resolving conflicts. It was where we learned some of the most valuable lessons, right there on the rough streets, under the wide-open Florida sky.

Summer camp was off the table, my mama couldn't afford it and getting around wasn't exactly a breeze. She couldn't even line up for the subsidized programs. But let me tell you, that didn't put a damper on our summer vibes.

Our days were filled with treks to the beach, fishing, diving into the canal bank with fishing rod in hand, and trips to the Wilson pool and the Wilson Center. Summer camp, who needs that when you got your own version?

The Wilson Center dished out free bag lunches and we'd follow that up with a splash at the pool. Pool time done, we'd bounce off to play on that old, grimy mattress or to find a high-stakes marble game. We would end the day with a game of football, two hand touch, or tackle in the grass.

The days we skipped the pool and the center, we'd hunker down at the canal with our fishing rods. Once we had our buckets filled with fish, we'd jump into the water.

Thinking back now, it's wild that we'd dive into a canal where gators, snakes, you name it, was probably in there.

But we were just kids, fear was a foreign concept, all we cared about was that rush of fun.

Those times, those struggles, they taught us the value of hustle. It wasn't just about making ends meet, it was about finding joy in the hustle, about learning that even when life gives you a tough hand, you can still play a good game.

As I reflect today on my past experiences, I realize that despite the harsh realities, my childhood was a testament to the human spirit's resilience. We might have been poor, but we were rich in experiences, rich in love, and rich in community. We scraped through, making the best of what we had, never letting the struggle define us, always finding ways to mine joy from the mundane.

As I revisit the shadows of my early years, I'm struck by the indelible imprints those experiences left on my understanding of social and economic inequity.

Back in the 1980s, when Ronald Reagan presided over the White House and hip-hop music was beginning to shape our culture, my family and I were grappling with a less glamorous reality. Money, or the lack of it, was a constant hum in the background, an insidious specter that lurked in every decision, every aspiration, every dream we dared to harbor. Those days of fiscal adversity forged in me a profound and deeply personal comprehension of the systemic disparities that plague our society, coloring my perceptions and molding my identity into what it is today.

In my younger days, growing up on the unforgiving streets of hardship, I was more than just a witness to disparity—I was a living testament. As a young Black boy in the 'eighties, my life seemed to be bound by daunting statistics.

It's hard to imagine that in 1983, the U.S. Census Bureau reported that 35% of African Americans were trapped in the chains of poverty, a number almost triple that of our white counterparts. This wasn't just data on a sheet; it was the day-to-day narrative of my life.

My reality was a world filled with glaring absences—adequate healthcare was a seeming luxury, and educational institutions felt more like detention centers than places of enlightenment. Homes that often felt like mere stopovers, hastily set up defenses against life's relentless challenges. These weren't mere external factors—they were the dark hues coloring my early perceptions of societal imbalance.

This wasn't some abstract knowledge gleaned from books; it was the marrow-deep realization of what deprivation truly feels like. The world I knew was a world where the game seemed rigged from the starting line.

Yet, as unrelenting as these circumstances were, they carved into me an intimate understanding of life's imbalances. My lessons weren't confined to textbooks, they were the raw experiences of what it meant to claw one's way through life, always playing against a hand that seemed perpetually stacked. This intricate dance with adversity became a core part of who I was, influencing how I saw and moved within the world.

But from this crucible of shared hardship emerged a profound empathy. My journey fostered a kinship with others sailing similarly troubled seas—an empathy not born from mere pity but rooted in the shared adversity of life's battleground. It wasn't learned, it was lived, and its potency was all the sharper for it.

While my story carries the weight of challenges, it isn't chained by them. These formidable shadows ignited a fierce desire to transform the status quo, to rise above and beyond my beginnings. It wasn't just about overcoming my own challenges, it was about pushing for change, letting my story shine a light on the glaring inequalities that marked my younger days.

There were moments of reflection, moments when the bitterness would rise, when I'd question the unfairness of it all. Why were families like mine, especially so many Black families, ensnared in such relentless cycles? Why was my reality one of scraping by while others seemingly danced in abundance?

The gleaming shoes on other kids, their untouched school materials—they were constant reminders of the divide that lay between us. My modest surroundings, the no -brand garments, the hand-me-down furniture—they were relentless reflections of our straitened state. Moving from one ramshackle dwelling to another, belongings carried in mismatched containers—it was an ever-present sign of our financial confines.

Reflecting on those defining years, I recognize the molding pressures of my history. As a young Black boy braving the challenges of the 1980s, life was an unforgiving teacher. Yet, it was precisely this crucible that shaped my character, honing it on the anvil of adversity.

Life's harshest lessons, those grueling years, felt like being thrust into an inferno. Every hurdle, every sting of pain, intensified the heat, reshaping my essence and imbuing within me an unyielding spirit, resilient as the finest forged steel.

Starting in a world that seemed to play favorites, my early days were humble and testing. But it was this very backdrop that kindled an unquenchable thirst for change within me. My resolve mirrored the perpetual might of ocean waves, constantly crashing against shores only to return with renewed vigor. And much like those resilient waves, whenever life tried to ground me, I rallied back with even greater force, ready for the next challenge.

Necessity, they say, gives birth to innovation. In my narrative, it birthed unyielding tenacity. Growing up, valuing every single penny taught me the true weight of hard work, laying the foundation for my future achievements.

When abundance is a rarity, creativity flourishes. With limited resources and countless challenges, I mastered the dance of adaptability, unearthing solutions where none seemed to exist, and swiftly pivoting to meet life's ever-changing demands. These became my guiding principles, steering me through the tumultuous seas of existence.

Enduring the rough embrace of poverty, I gathered resilience in its rawest form. From unsettling brushes with crime and looming threats of violence to the uphill fight for basic amenities like education and health, each challenge was a testament to my indomitable spirit, reinforcing my resolve to persevere.

The sting of societal inequities, the structural shackles that perpetuated the cycle of poverty, awakened in me a fervent desire for change. Not just in my life, but in the lives of my family and the broader community. I became a challenger of the status quo, an agitator for progress, committed to breaking down the barriers that held us back. This potent motivation fuels my journey towards success and, I hope, will lead to a lasting, positive impact.

In retrospect, the trials of my youth distilled a wealth of lessons I believe are vital to share with those who may be grappling with the same demons that haunted me. Here are the truths I unearthed from my dance with scarcity.

The oppressive weight of poverty can grind away at your self-confidence, shrouding you in a cloak of self-doubt and hopelessness. But remember this:

- Your circumstances are not a measure of your worth or your potential.

- Don't let what you're going through define who you are.

- You are a beacon of potential, so hold fast to the belief that you are capable of greatness.

- If you don't believe in yourself, convincing others to do so is an uphill battle.

Education isn't just a steppingstone, it's an escalator to a better future. It can provide the leverage needed to pry open the heavy doors of poverty. So, grasp that hunger for knowledge with both hands and never let go. Education is more than a key—it's a master key that can unlock doors you've only dared to dream of.

Crossing the unstable territory of poverty can feel like navigating a minefield, but the journey can be less intimidating with a guide. Don't hesitate to seek mentorship or support. Whether from a role model whose footsteps you aspire to follow, a community leader, or a supportive organization, their wisdom and guidance can help illuminate your path.

The relentless grind of poverty necessitates an extra dose of grit and perseverance. Embrace this necessity. The hand you're dealt in life isn't as important as how you play it.

Never underestimate the power of sharing your victories with your community. If you've scaled the steep cliffs of poverty, consider reaching back to help others make the same climb. Pour your successes back into the community that shaped you. Your skills, resources, and experiences are not just your triumphs, they are tools that can uplift and empower others on their own journeys.

I'd say to my younger self, and to any young soul grappling with the struggle, "You are not defined by your circumstances, but by the decisions you make. Your choices will shape your future, so choose wisely."

Reflecting on my past, I now see the veins of silver that threaded through the darkness of my childhood poverty. Those were lessons in resilience and grit, each one hard earned and valuable beyond measure.

Poverty, for all its brutal harshness, was an unforgiving teacher of resilience. It was like growing up in a storm, facing challenges and obstacles that hit like gusts of wind, relentless and battering. But every setback was a lesson in endurance, in the art of bending without breaking. It was there, in the thick of it that I learned to face adversity head-on, to dust myself off and move forward, no matter the odds stacked against me.

Scarcity, the constant companion of poverty, was my crucible for creativity. With resources as sparse as water in a desert, I was forced to think outside the box, to devise solutions that others might overlook. I learned to stretch each dollar, to make do and mend, to repurpose and recycle. I became adept at finding unconventional routes to meet my needs and achieve my goals, a skill that served me well in later life.

If there's one thing poverty ignites in you, it's a fire, a burning ambition to rise above the circumstances you were born into. I can attest to this, for it was poverty that sparked a drive in me, a relentless motivation to better my life and those of my family. It instilled a hustle in me, a tenacity to work hard, seize opportunities, and relentlessly pursue success.

Contrary to what you might think, poverty also taught me the art of appreciation. I learned to savor even the smallest victories, to cherish modest advancements. Inner city Black boys like me, who wrestled with the chains of poverty, often develop a keen sense of gratitude for every forward step, no matter how seemingly insignificant. And it's this mindset, this ability to find fulfillment in the 'small wins', that contributes to a more optimistic outlook on life.

Growing up in poverty does more than just toughen you up, it softens your heart. It nurtures a deep-seated empathy and compassion in you, a firsthand understanding of the struggles that others in similar situations face. This understanding has spurred me to extend a helping hand, to advocate for those less fortunate, to become a beacon in my community, and to uplift others who are still trapped in the cycle of poverty.

These strengths and virtues, born from the poverty I lived through became the driving forces behind my character, my perspectives, and my actions. They were the building blocks for my personal growth, resilience, and unwavering determination to carve out a better future for myself and those who come after me.

PART TWO
Rising Above

Chapter Three
Delinquency: a detour not a destiny

"… believe me when I tell you, you're stronger than the trials you face."

Alright, let's get into it. This is the part where shit got real, where young Ricky was trippin', caught up in the life of juvenile delinquency.

Picture me, young and wild, crossing lines, testing boundaries, thinking I was slicker than grease. But see, the thing about that life and that way of thinking is it's quick to catch up with you, and before I knew it, I was waist-deep in trouble.

This ain't my proudest moment, actually its far from it. But it was a time of reckoning, a crossroads that started to twist my path in unexpected directions. I was a hot-headed youngster making a mess of things, but life wasn't done teaching me lessons. My ride through the madness of delinquency was just a prelude, setting me up for the wakeup call I didn't know I needed.

Through all the chaos, there were some real ones who stepped up, folks who saw through my tough-guy act and recognized a kid lost in the system. These mentors threw me a lifeline, guiding me, schooling me when I needed it most. My journey through juvenile delinquency was one hell of a rollercoaster ride, but it played a huge part in molding me into the man I am today. So, buckle up, 'cause we're about to dive headfirst into the gritty details of my clash with the law and how it changed the game for your boy.

There's a special kind of anguish that hits you when your dreams feel like pipe dreams. When you're a young brother growing up in a neighborhood that treats tomorrow like a gamble, not a guarantee. For real, there were days when my young self couldn't fathom a world where I'd see my 21st birthday. The world was too gritty, too unforgiving, and here I was, just a kid knee-deep in it all.

In those years, survival wasn't just a concept, it was a lifeline. From the moment I could understand the value of a dollar, I was out there hustling. First, it was selling candy in 4th grade, then selling newspaper subscriptions for the Palm Beach Post, our local newspaper. It didn't take long before the harsh reality of my circumstances pushed me into a world, I had no business knowing, the world of drug dealing. Yeah, your boy Ricky wasn't just peddling candy anymore. I was out there selling weed and crack cocaine, the cooked white poison that turned vibrant communities into ghost towns.

You might be wondering, "How did a kid like Ricky fall into that life?" The answer's simple—survival and desperation, man. It started when dreams seemed like illusions, far -off fantasies that had no place in a world as raw as mine. Thinking about the future was a luxury, something that felt out of place when each day was a struggle in its own right.

Money became my ticket to a semblance of respect, a way to feel significant in a world that seemed intent on keeping me down. And so, I hustled. I graduated from selling newspaper subscriptions, candy, weed, and then, almost inevitably, crack.

Back in middle school, me and my friends found ourselves stuck in that old dilemma, how to make a buck. Now, I ain't talkin' about pocket change, I mean real money, the kind that can make a difference in your life.

The joke-cracking and fighting that used to fill our days had given way to a hustle mentality, and we found our answer in candy and cookies, a sweet business that gave us the first taste of financial freedom. Afterwards, we'd go door to door, peddling subscriptions to the Palm Beach Post, and by God's grace, we made it work. Our eyes were set on a trip to Disney World the newspaper was offering. We'd tell folks that their newspaper subscriptions would make it happen. We weren't just sellin' subscriptions, we were sellin' dreams.

As the customers subscribed, I started raking in money, and the taste of it was better than any candy we sold. Soon, I began to see the potential in investments, understanding even then the importance of putting money to work. I knew the job was temporary and it was important for me to plan ahead.

I turned the newspaper money into candy money, and the school halls became my marketplace. Airheads, Blow Pops, and Jolly Ranchers – those were my products, and they sold like hotcakes. The money flowed, and I went from wearing no name, worn-out shoes to the name brand stuff like Converse, Nike, and Air Jordan. I was a young entrepreneur, thriving on ambition.

Middle school was a new world filled with opportunities and risks. I expanded my product line, dealing with different people, even providing opportunities for friends to work for me, all while learning the ins and outs of the game. But my hustle didn't go unnoticed and was highly respected.

One time, my flashy display of cash got me into hot water. The principal called me down, brought the police in, and they tried to crack me, no pun intended, thinking I was pushing drugs. They couldn't fathom a young Black kid making an honest dollar. I held my ground, telling them it was just candy, and the money was from my mama. They didn't believe me, but I stuck to my story. It took my mama telling them she gave me the money for them to let up.

As time went on, I found myself drifting into darker territory. I found myself becoming a product of my environment. There were more illegal than legal opportunities for a young man like me, at least, that's what I thought. I had very little to lose and everything to gain. Weed became part of the game, then crack, introduced by a good friend.

I vividly remember the night I sold my first rocks, standing on the streets of Boynton Beach, eyes wide open to a new world. The money was fast and addictive, and it pulled me deeper into the game.

The turning point came when one of my good friends, Jay and I sold to an undercover cop. We had been making plays all day and we were down to our last few rocks. We were riding on 4th Ave, and a white dude in a green car flagged us down, asking for "dope." Nervous but hungry for the sale, we made the deal, only to realize too late that it was a set up and we'd sold to an undercover cop.

Panic set in as the police descended upon us. They slammed me and my friend to the ground and roughed us up. They took our money, charged us with selling cocaine, and just like that, my world came crashing down.

I was only thirteen, but I felt a lifetime older, bearing the weight of my choices and the crushing realization that I'd been caught up in a game I couldn't win. The sale charge was another one of my legal troubles, and my life was about to take a turn down a path I hadn't intended.

Through it all, those memories of fourth-grade hustling, selling candy, and dreaming big remained, a haunting reminder of innocence lost, and lessons learned the hard way.

Let me tell you about this crazy shit that went down during my juvenile delinquent years. Back then, I was wild, full of youthful recklessness, thinking I was invincible or some shit. So, one day, I'm chillin' at home, not in school when I should have been, when one of my boys come up to me.

"Hey, Ricky," he says, his eyes gleaming with that mischievous look that only kids can have, "you want to go pull a lick?"

I was like, "Hell yeah!" The prospect of a "come up" was too good to pass up. So, we headed to this house down the street, a place that looked ripe for the come up. We broke in, just like that. Shoes, a BB gun, Sega Genesis game, jewelry, money, and all kinds of shit. We grabbed what we could. It felt like some kind of victory, like we'd just hit the jackpot.

I took what I wanted from the lick and headed home, feeling like a king. My sister and her friend were home from school, playing some games or whatever, and they kept messin' with me all day, saying, "Hey, the police are here!" Shit like that.

I was messin' with them too, crackin' jokes and whatnot, so when they started with that police talk again, I was like, "Stop playing." But they were serious this time.

"Ricky, the police are out here. We're not playing this time," insisted my sister. "The police are out here."

I was in the shower, so I thought, 'Okay, let me come out and see what's going on.' I came out with just my towel on, feeling all big and bold.

The officer was looking all stern and official. "Is Seaweed here?" the officer asked, referring to my cousin by his nickname. "Nah, he ain't here," I told the officer.

The officer continued, "Well, this guy says there are stolen goods in your home. Do you mind if I come in?"

I'm thinkin', 'Shit, this is real!' "Okay, let me just put on some shorts right quick," I answered.

The officer came in, spotted the stolen goods, and just took them, cool as you please. As I watched him, I was feeling like a damn fool, knowing I was caught.

Then he asked me to step outside, and there in the back of the police car was my so-called friend, grinning like a

damn Cheshire cat, laughing and pointing, like, "Yeah, that's him."

They got me. Just like that, my moment of triumph turned to ashes in my mouth. They took me to jail and slapped a charge on me. That was a wake-up call, a taste of reality that I'll never forget.

It wasn't my first run-in with the law, but it was a moment that stuck with me, a lesson learned in the unforgiving school of life. The thrill of the heist, the camaraderie of my friends, and the cold, hard truth of consequences. All of it wrapped up in a memory that I carry with me. A reminder of where I've been and how far I've come. You see, back during those days, I had many run-ins with the law.

Let me take you back to the time when things really started getting wild. I'm talking about a young and foolish thirteen-year-old me, just gettin' tangled up in all sorts of crazy shit. This ain't no fairy tale, this was real life, living on the edge, where every decision could lead you down a dark path.

I remember the old Winn-Dixie grocery store on Federal Highway in Boynton Beach. In the same plaza was a men's clothing store and a store that sold beepers.

Every day, my cousin and I would walk to the beach, passing the beeper store. The store's glass would be shimmering in the sunlight, promising treasures hidden inside.

One day, I turned to my cousin and said, "I think we could break in there." Every damn day we walked by, on our way to the beach that thought kept gnawing at me, until it became an obsession.

One night, my friends and I, full of youthful arrogance, decided we could do it. We took out the jalousie windowpanes that night and lifted my cousin up through the window. I can still feel the adrenaline pumping as he swung open the back door, his face lit up, whispering, "Guess what, it's open!"

We ran back, our hearts pounding, only to be met by the wailing of police sirens. The police started chasing my cousin and another friend, their blue lights flashing, cutting through the dark night.

But while they were occupied, me and my other friend slipped inside the store, grabbing everything we could. We broke things, we made a mess, and then we ran home, the police hot on our heels. But we got away, hiding our loot, and returning the next day to claim it.

My aunt had to go down to the police station to get my cousin. There was pressure, accusations, and finally, they caught up to me too. They charged us with so much because we'd taken so much.

We were selling beepers, hustling like we were some damn businessmen. Well, we were businessmen, just not the legal kind. But there were consequences. The restitution that I had to pay back was ridiculous. And I was only thirteen.

But that wasn't all. There was more trouble. I was robbing folks, pulling licks with my uncle, Mom's brother. I was doing all kinds of shady shit with him. Sometimes we were short on rent money, and my auntie would be like,

"We need to get this rent money. What are you all going to do?"

"Don't worry about it, Auntie, we got it." Our solution was to rob people, just like that, to keep a roof over our heads.

My mom was working hard, doing the kind of work folks don't appreciate, like working at Motel 6 as a housekeeper. But we had to do what we had to do, hustling, making money in ways we shouldn't.

By the time I was 14 or 15, the game had changed. Me and my buddies, playing football together, got introduced to stealing cars. We'd steal cars and go joyriding, going to block parties, only to get into more trouble.

The reckless abandon of youth, the thrill of the police chases, the constant battle with right and wrong—it all shaped me, leaving scars that run deep. Looking back, I see a young man trying to survive, making choices out of desperation, caught in a cycle of chaos and crime.

Now, I want to take you back to the local skating rink, where shit always went down. We'd start fights at the skating rink, just to prove who was the toughest. You had to represent

Boynton, our hometown. You had to stand tall, show what you were made of.

The craziness didn't stop there. In the daytime, we'd ride bicycles and go looking for a fight, just to see who had the hardest knockout blow. It was like a game to us. Except this game was raw, and brutal. We would also have foot races to see who was the fastest, and then when the night came, oh man, the night.

We'd steal cars and joy ride in them like they were our own. I ain't proud of it, but we developed a name and reputation in the hood. People knew they could buy parts from us. We'd steal a car, break it down, and then sell the parts to whoever needed them. Rims and car stereo systems were always hot items. At times we'd have so many radios and speakers at my friend's house, it looked like a pawn shop.

Have you ever been in a high-speed chase? I mean a real one, not some movie shit. We would take the stolen cars, and we'd be racing, chased by cops on I-95 all the way to Miami sometimes. Helicopters overhead, sirens blaring, heart beating like a damn drum. We were young and dumb, thuggin without a care in the world.

I'm going to keep it a 100 and continue to be honest. We had a wild crew that was down for whatever whenever. When

I say that, I mean it literally. There was one night, we were out joyriding looking for another "lick," a come up. It was early morning, around 3 am.

As we rode, we saw this dude on the corner. He's decked out, wearing a nice chain, bracelet, and his pockets looked full. Driving past, we recognized him from school. He was clearly on the wrong side of town, the wrong time of night.

We scoped out the scene, masked up and pulled up on him. "You know the drill playboy, lay the fuck down!" We robbed him, took his gold chain, bracelet, watch, and cash. It was a sweet lil lick because we knew he was soft as cotton and wasn't going to call the police.

The following week, we were in school having lunch and the dude we had robbed was sharing his version of how he was robbed. He fabricated the whole story, and it was funny hearing him lie about what had actually happened. He's talking big, $3000 in cash, a Rolex watch. Me and my boy Spot just exchanged a look and tried not to crack up. The reality was a measly $600, a Timex watch and bracelet.

I often think about telling buddy about the situation, and who knows, one day I just might. I can honestly say, we were really wild in the streets acting a fool.

But then one day, it hit me. I thought to myself. I'm not a thief, and I'm no thug. 'Ricky, you're a hustler!' Why are you out here stealing cars? Why are you robbing folks? This isn't you. I quickly realized the trouble that I was getting into was no longer worth the risk.

After being in and out of detention centers, I started to pull away from that life. I went into a court-ordered level 6 program for delinquents. These were my steps away from that dark path. I was fifteen, and I'd already seen enough to last a lifetime.

Now, my mama, bless her heart, she was seeing this dude that I didn't like. Between you and me, I couldn't stand his fuck ass. The dude was full of shit. Always running his mouth with some lie or another. Like, he'd tell my mama he paid a bill when he didn't, or he'd flex like he's some big man when we all knew he was just all talk.

One thing that really set me off was when I thought he tried to lay hands on my sister. Nah, man. Not on my watch. You don't mess with my blood. He'd say slick shit to my mom too, thinking I wouldn't hear. But I heard it all.

I was wild as a juvenile, I was fifteen, just a year before my son came into this world and living in this cramped one-bedroom apartment. That's when I bought my first piece, a

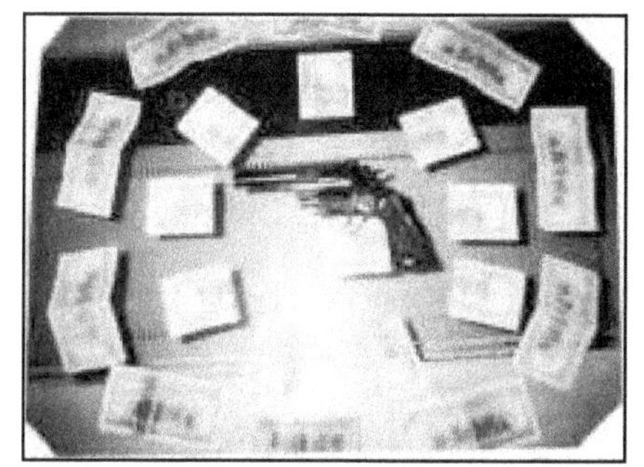

little deuce deuce, a .22 caliber pistol, from this older cat I knew. Crazy part? The only place I could stash it was under my mama's bed. Yeah, I know. Wild, right? Every time I got in some trouble or felt like blowing off steam, I'd grab that gun and take some shots outside.

But then, this one night, my mama boyfriend, the dude I didn't like, pissed me off really bad. I was ready to end him. In my head I had planned out the situation and how I was going to knock him off. The bed where he slept was near the window, "Man, it'd be so easy. Just one shot." But when I went to get my piece to finish him, it was gone. Damn!

Imagine the awkwardness, right? Trying to ask my mama if she'd seen my gun. But I mustered up the courage. "Hey umm, Mama, you seen a gun under your bed?" She was heated, of course. But then her boyfriend chimed in, all smug.

"Yeah, I saw it. I took it straight to the police station 'cause your young ass don't need to be messing with no damn guns."

I knew he was full of shit. Dude had a habit of pawning things. I knew the plays he was on. So, I hit the pawn shop and what do I find? My damn gun, right there in the glass case. He pawned it! Talkin' about he took it to the police.

Man, whatever!

Now, looking back, I'm kinda glad he took that gun. Had he not, he would've been a dead man and I would've been in prison. Everyone in my family knew how I felt about him, especially after that incident with my sister. But fate has its ways, you know? Life's funny like that.

I started to focus on my hustle, selling drugs, but smarter. I wasn't just some corner boy; I was building clientele. I was dealing with higher-end folks, spending time with my girl and leaving that car-stealing and wild life behind. And damn, was I glad I did.

Watching my old friends get jammed up, seeing people get shot right in front of my face, like the world was spiraling out of control. I saw multiple people shot and killed right before my eyes, one guy's whole side blown out, gone, just like that. Many of my close friends were shot and some even lost their lives to gun violence.

This was real life, a whirlwind of violence and chaos, where every decision could lead to death or jail. But I made it out. Many of the people I used to run with ended up with some serious prison time. I'm talking about twenty-five plus years and some of them with life sentences with no possibility of getting out.

Speaking of long sentences, one of my childhood friends, known as Fella, was sentenced to a long bid. Fella was a muthafucka in the streets. He was always down to pull a lick to get some cash. It was an everyday thing for us back then. You couldn't tell us that crime didn't pay because it paid us well. Thank God for change because unfortunately for Fella, he ended up catching a 30-year sentence.

Although he was locked up, our friendship always remained strong. I communicated with him often, but prior to my first visit with him, I had not seen him in years. As soon as we saw each other we went in on each other cracking jokes. Then we talked and played cards and checkers for a few hours. We reminisced on old times, old crimes, and cracked more jokes.

I know many people behind those walls and the system really broke them mentally. Not Fella, he maintained his mental health and always had a good attitude. It was good to hear him talk about the positive moves he was making inside those walls and his plans for when he returns home.

It takes a true soldier to keep your head up and smile through those circumstances. As I was sitting there, I realized that I could've easily been where he is, and he could have been where I am. We both were from the same hood, jumped on the same dirty mattresses, played sports, and were involved in crime together. I was only one crime away from being in his shoes. I'm so grateful for the change in the path I chose because I could have been doing serious time just as many of my homies.

I'm thankful that part of my life is behind me now. It shaped me, gave me hard-earned lessons that I've never forgotten. It's a world that lingers in the shadows of my memory, a time of danger and desperation, where every day was a gamble, every choice a crossroad.

It's a story of survival, of a young man finding his way through a maze of violence and vice, learning to navigate the streets with a hustler's wisdom and a fighter's heart. A tale of redemption, of leaving behind a world of crime, and finding a path toward something better, something real.

These were the gritty streets that raised me, taught me hard lessons, and forced me to grow up fast. A world where innocence was a luxury and survival was the only goal. A time when life was a series of blurred lines and dangerous games, a narrative created from mistakes and triumphs, and the enduring will to keep moving forward.

Ain't no glory in that life, but there's truth, and there's growth. It's a chapter I've closed, but the memories linger, a reminder of where I've been and how far I've come. It's a past that's shaped me, but it doesn't define me. When I look back at all the poor choices I made out of the need to survive, I think back to those people who believed in me when my world seemed nothing but a foggy haze. I'm flooded with gratitude.

Mr. Richard Rathel stands out distinctly. I met him in one of those Department of Juvenile Justice programs I was funneled into. He wasn't just some staff member there, he was a ray of hope. His voice was like a cool breeze on a summer afternoon, calming and reassuring. Every conversation with him left me with a nugget of wisdom and a spark of hope. He became my touchstone, always available, always offering a listening ear, even when I left the program. He planted the seed of aspiration in me, asking me to envision a life where I could be in his shoes, reaching out to help others.

And then there was Ms. Fredericks, another gem from the system. Her check-ins weren't mere formalities, they were lifelines. She had this remarkable way of making me feel seen and valued, constantly reminding me that I was meant for more. "Ricky, this ain't you," she'd say with earnestness in her eyes. And I believed her.

Vontell Mills was another such angel. She was like a mother to me, exposing me to experiences beyond my wildest dreams. Through her, I discovered faith, which became an anchor in my tumultuous life. To this day, when I think of Christmas, I remember her kindness. And despite her humble living situation, to me, she was the richest person I knew— not in wealth, but in heart.

Ms. Jessie Lee Anderson was another godsend. Our bond began in the most unexpected way. I was a curious kid eyeing her mango tree, and she was the stern yet caring woman admonishing me. But from that chance encounter, we forged a bond that went deeper than familial ties. She was my rock, a voice of reason, teaching me the true essence of discipline.

And throughout my school years, there was Ms. Maxine Perry. She saw past my teenage rebelliousness and recognized my potential, pushing me towards academic excellence and encouraging me to set my sights on Bethune -Cookman College. She was my guiding star, illuminating the path of education and resilience.

Bill Tome also left an indelible mark. As a cop, he could've been just another figure of authority. But he chose to be more.

Through the Police Athletic League program, he reached out, teaching me and many others discipline and teamwork, and most importantly, giving us hope.

Looking back, I realize that my journey was filled with silent heroes. From Mr. Kouf, my fifth-grade teacher, to the late Ms. Jessie and the ever-inspiring Ms. Mills. They not only believed in me but instilled in me values that I cherish to this day.

Ms. Mills, with her unwavering faith, taught me the power of unconditional love and the importance of community service. Ms. Perry instilled in me the tenacity to overcome challenges, while Ms. Jessie, with her no-nonsense approach, taught me the importance of discipline and structure. I remember her reaction to my flashy earring. A sharp rebuke followed by a lesson in self-respect.

Mr. Leon Jenkins, our landlord and my middle school gym coach, created a program for young men at the school. He taught us the importance of unity, teamwork and not giving up. He took us on trips and to my first Miami Heat game. He not only told us he cared about us, but he showed us as well.

Each of these incredible souls touched my life in unique ways, molding me into the man I am today. Their belief in me was the hope I needed in my darkest hours. And while I might've strayed a few times, their faith pulled me back, teaching me the most important lesson of all – no matter where you come from, with the right guidance, you can always find your way.

To all you young kings and queens out there, walking the tightrope of life's challenges, I've been where you stand, feeling the weight of the world pressing down. I know the alleys you wander, the shadows you dodge. But believe me when I tell you, you're stronger than the trials you face. I've been blessed to have angels in my corner, guiding me when I was on the brink, and you too will find those guiding lights in your life. Hold onto hope, even when it feels like a flickering candle in a gusty wind.

Remember, every storm you weather, every mountain you climb, shapes the resilient soul inside you. You're meant for greatness, and no circumstance can dim the brilliance that is your birthright. Lean on those who believe in you, learn from your past, and step boldly into the future that's waiting. Like me, you have the strength and the spirit to rise above. Stay the course, and let your journey be a testament to the world.

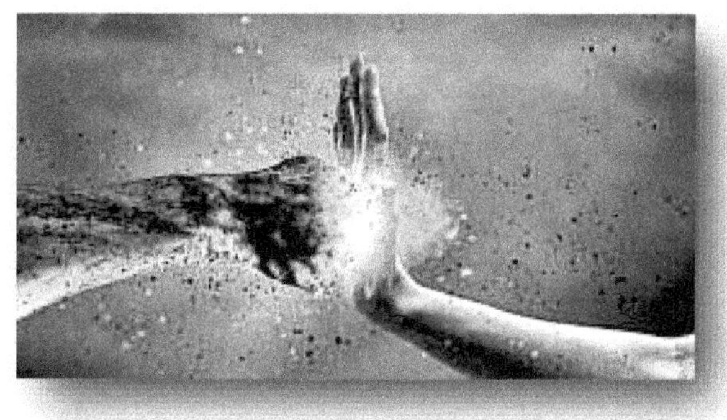

Chapter Four
Early Fatherhood

"I desired to be the ever-present father figure I never had."

At sixteen, when most of my peers were juggling homework and weekend plans, I found myself navigating a path lined with baby bottles, sleepless nights, and the harsh weight of responsibility that no boy is truly prepared for. But this wasn't just about being a teen parent. This was a juncture in my journey, coming hot on the heels of my periods with juvenile delinquency.

Life was handing me a second chance, wrapped up in the soft coos and delicate fingers of a child of my own. This chapter, my friends, is a testament to the steep mountains I had to climb, the valleys of despair I sometimes found myself in, and the surprising joys of young fatherhood. It's about finding growth in unexpected places, rediscovering purpose, and understanding that sometimes, our biggest trials shape our grandest triumphs.

When I first learned my girl was expecting, it was a surreal moment. The news hit me like a freight train. My girlfriend was pregnant! At the time, I had a lot going on, navigating the maze that was our young relationship.

Immediately, expectations and responsibilities took on new, hefty meanings. I was expected to provide food on the table and to wade through the stormy seas of her fluctuating emotions. My patience, always a part of my identity, was tested daily. Yet, I was adaptable, resilient. My financial acumen had me hustling hard, ensuring money was never a problem.

So, let me break this down for you. At first, all of it felt like a damn illusion, like one of those too-good-to-be-true moments. Was this shit for real? I mean, it ain't everyday you wrap your head around the fact you got a little one on the way. But as her belly started to grow, man, reality hit me like a freight train. Like, "Damn, is this actually happening?" It wasn't just talk anymore, you feel me?

I remember it vividly. My girlfriend, my high school sweetheart had just returned to Boynton Beach from living in Jacksonville for nearly a year. We missed each other so much. I began to stay overnight at her mother's home, and we spent a lot of time together. Don't get it twisted, although I was allowed to stay the night at her mother's home, I was not allowed to sleep in her bedroom.

Of course, being a young man, I would sneak in her room every chance I got. At one point, I got bold enough to write her mom a letter explaining why she should allow me to sleep in the room with her daughter, my girlfriend. I guess the years of learning to negotiate gave me the nerve I needed. After reading the letter, her mother responded. "You are a lil bold mutherfucker!" she said and we both chuckled.

Her mother, my Momma Joe, was a sweet, fun-loving mother. She knew we had been intimate and had the talk with her about birth control. She took her to the doctor, and she received her prescription for birth control pills. The doctor informed her to begin taking the pills after her next period. Well, her next period never came.

It's funny how life plays out. She misses her cycle, comes up to me with those big eyes and announces, "I'm pregnant!" I looked at her, almost laughing,

"You jokin', right? Nah, stop playing." But deep down, I had this gut feeling. 'This ain't no joke,' I thought to myself. She took a couple of weeks before she got the nerve to tell her mama. I kept nudging her to say something. "Look, you gotta tell your moms. This ain't something to play with."

We sat down, both still kids ourselves, thinking about what's next. Abortion? Man, I don't know. I've always believed in a woman's right to choose, but it felt different because it was my own blood. It's not like she was dead set on it, but it was a conversation. A heavy one, at that.

When her mama found out, she gave it to us straight. Sat us down, real talk, no sugar-coating. She basically told us, "Y'all made this bed, now lie in it." In other words, step up and handle your business. Be parents. So, that's where we were. Life, man, it comes at you fast.

So, let's take it back to 1996, that's when the shit got real. Me and my girlfriend have birthdays that are a day apart, January 23rd and 24th. It's wild, right? We were probably deep in it around that time, yet everything was a whirlwind. I ain't gonna lie, it didn't feel real. 'Am I really gonna be a daddy now?'

But I stepped up. I wasn't about to be like the dude that helped conceive me, missing out on everything. Nah, I was gonna be there for every damn step, every laugh, every score, and every tear. I wanted to see it all.

Well, when I broke it to my mom, she thought I was joking. She was looking at me sideways and laughing. "Boy, you trippin'. Are you for real?" But once the initial shock wore off, she got real.

"You need a job, son. Gotta step up now." With that being said, it hit me.

'She's right,' I thought. Plus, with juvenile probation hanging over my head, work wasn't just a good idea, it was a damn necessity.

So, there I was, flipping roast beef at Arby's, part-time. It was just a couple of days a week, but I was making ends meet and keeping the probation officer off my back. Life was coming at me fast, but I did what I had to do.

I gotta say, the heaviest part while she was expecting was juggling it all—school, sports, doctors' visits, work, and the whole nine yards. But then this angel, Mrs. Rita Simmons, came into our lives. She was always involved with helping young people and she connected us with a program designed for teen parents. She would sit us down, me and my girl, and school us on how to handle our new reality. She was a godsend.

We also enrolled in classes at the school, tailored for teen parents like us. We quickly found out we weren't the only young couples expecting. There were others on the same journey. I believe the program was an initiative of a non-profit organization known as "Healthy Mothers, Healthy Babies." They had our backs. They provided resources, guidance – the whole shebang.

Now, here's where the juggling act got tricky. I had managed to get my grades on track, and I was itching to hit the football field again. So, imagine trying to keep up with practice, show up for my girl, and hustle to make sure we had what we needed. Man, it was a trip.

But the silver lining was my mother. She held me down, 100%. She didn't just support us emotionally but stepped in big time when Ricky Jr. arrived. My mom, bless her heart, even put her job on pause to watch over our little guy, making sure we could finish school. Now that's love.

Unfortunately, my girl caught a ton of criticism from her folks. "She's movin' too fast," some said. "That side of the family is always up to something," said others. I felt like she had it harder. Women, especially young ones, always seem to catch more heat.

And me being young, whenever I dropped the news, folks would hit me with that wide-eyed look of disbelief. It made me second-guess every time I had to share. Some of the adults threw me those sideways glances. Like, can a young brother not step up?

Then there was George, one of my homeboys. Funny thing was, he was in the same boat but was keeping it on the low, just like me. One day he goes, "Man, Ricky, guess what?" And I'm like, "What's good?" He hits me with, "I'm about to be a dad." I'm thinking he's pulling my leg. But nah, he was for real.

I said, "Man, speaking of babies, guess who else gonna be a dad?" We laughed about it, even talked about names for our babies.

George was like, "if I have a boy, his name will be George, Jr. I said that if I have a son, his name would be Ricky, Jr. There always need to be a Ricky Petty gracing this earth.

But then George threw a curveball at me. "What if you have a girl?" I told him if I had a girl, her name would be Rickia. He then said if he had a girl, he would name his daughter Gekia. Funny enough, I had a son, and he had a daughter. Kept my word, named my boy Ricky Jr. And when I did have a daughter, I named her Rickia, just like I said. All my children's names will begin with the letter "R" and my second daughter's name is Rickiya. I guess that's just me being Petty.

Man, it was wild. My friend, Jay dropped the baby bomb around the same time. Felt like all of us were entering fatherhood together. Young dads, just trying to navigate.

Man, you ever get hit with that doubt? That gnawing feeling? As a young buck, my mind was racing. 'Is this kid really mine?' I started thinking. My girl swore up and down that it was. "It's only ever been you, baby," She insisted. But the player in me was skeptical.

"Come on now, you sure about that?" I asked. Although she never gave me a reason to feel doubtful, when you are young minded with this new experience, doubt crosses your mind. Questioning her like that, it hurt her deeply, made her think I was playing her.

At some point, I had to trust, but those feelings of uncertainty eat at you. Still, even with that on my mind, I stepped up. Late-night cravings? I was on it. Whatever she wanted, be it seafood, chicken, cookies, cakes you name it, I'd dash out to get it. Setting up a fly baby shower, ensuring she was comfortable—I did all that while juggling football, school, and everything else.

Then came the moment of truth. Holding that tiny life, cutting the umbilical cord, that's when it hits you. This ain't just real, it's a miracle. There he was my flesh and blood. A handsome baby boy weighing just a little over 5 lbs. It was one of my proudest moments. It was a great feeling and it felt surreal. Wow, I became a dad! But then I heard about the kidney issue. Man, life's never simple, is it?

Throughout it all, I had the unwavering support of my mother. She was the rock, the anchor. As I mentioned, she dropped everything, even her job, to ensure that our child, Ricky Jr., would have the best care possible. This wasn't a journey we traversed alone. There were whispers and judgment but love and hope prevailed. I wanted more for Ricky Jr. I desired to be the ever-present father figure I never had.

And then, when Ricky Jr. was born, new challenges surfaced. There were medical complications, nights at the hospital, and moments of helplessness. But every hurdle strengthened my resolve to be a better man, a better father.

Being older and wiser now, it's not often I feel like I'm fresh out of answers. But that day? That damn day was one for the books. My heart was heavy, man, like an anchor weighed down with all the pain and frustration in the world. Every cry from my baby felt like a sharp knife twisting in my gut. I felt paralyzed. Here I am, supposed to be this strong father figure, and there ain't shit I can do.

Watching the doctor mess up, as he was poking my boy over and over. I wasn't having it. "What the hell is this shit?!" I snapped, my voice sharp and laced with anger.

"Man, fuck this! You can't be playing around with my kid like that! Either you know what the fuck you're doing, or you don't! Bring someone who's got their shit together!" I may have been young, but damn if I was gonna let them torture my son like that.

Every wail from my boy, every tear he shed, it felt like a storm raging inside of me. And what could I do? Just stand there? Felt like a damn punch to the gut.

Then they dropped the news on me that they gotta keep him overnight because of that yellow jaundice thing. I swear to God, that moment dragged on like eternity. But once they cleared him of that, it was like the sun breaking through the darkest storm clouds. We finally got to take our boy home, where he belonged, and start our journey right.

From a young 16-year-old trying to wrap my head around being a daddy, I made sure things took a different route for my boy. You see, my old man wasn't around for me, and I swore I'd be constant in my son's life. Sports? Man, I was right there, not just cheering but coaching him through. Football, basketball, I was that dad. Active, present, and always involved.

I held it down at his school by participating with the PTA, coaching his basketball and football teams from the age of five until high school. Around the age of 6 or 7, he started pulling away from football and began to focus on basketball. Still, every year, I was there, at the community center, coaching, guiding, cheering the young ones on.

Football? Man, he wasn't really into it, he played only two years, but guess who was there, coaching? Yours truly. Even though the game meant more to me than it did to him. I was all fire and passion. To me, football was everything. My boy was with the Bulldogs, my old team, and my pride soared. But one day, his mama pulled me aside. "Ricky, you gotta face it. The boy ain't feeling football. His heart ain't in it." She talked about how he'd complain, how he didn't want to be out there. Man, that hit me deep.

I thought about the time, the money, the effort. I was crushed, but I told him to finish the season, after that, it's your call. And true to his word, once the season wrapped up, football was history. He took to the basketball court and never looked back. But you know, it's all good. It was about supporting him, letting him find his groove. And no matter the game, I was right there, coach's cap on, cheering my boy on. He played on the travel teams and in high school. He enjoyed the game and had so much love for the sport.

Being a teen father with a juvenile record hanging over my head wasn't an easy journey. Every step was like walking on a tightrope, teetering between the weight of my past and the hope for my son's future. Life threw its punches, and some were heavy, but my spirit was unbreakable. No challenge is too big when you got that fire in your soul. See, when I looked into my boy's eyes, I saw more than just a reflection of me, I saw a future, a promise, a challenge I was ready to take head-on.

It wasn't just about proving the naysayers wrong or outrunning my past, it was about giving my boy the life and support I never had. A father's presence, guidance, and love—things I craved growing up.

I made my share of mistakes, but with every stumble, my determination to be a rock for my son strengthened. The love of basketball, the coaching days, the heartbreaks of football, his education, they're more than memories, they're lessons, they're bonds. They represent my commitment to stay in my son's life.

In the grand scheme of life, being a teen dad with a juvenile criminal record might seem like a setback, but it was my motivation, my drive. It made me hungry to rewrite my narrative, to show my son and the world that our past doesn't define us, but how we rise above it does. My journey as a father wasn't just about being there for the basketball games or the school meetings, it was about being there, period. In heart, in spirit, every damn day!

So, to all the young dads out there, especially those with a past that feels like a mountain, remember this. The climb might be steep, but at the summit, the view is worth every damn struggle. Stay the course for your kids, and for yourself. The legacy you leave behind will echo for generations.

Keep pushing, keep loving, and always, always be present.

Chapter Five
The Power of Sports

Alright, let's talk about the game, not just the one on the field, but the game of life. If there's one thing that molded me, shaped my spirit, and gave me structure on this wild journey, it was the power of sports. Baseball, basketball, and football, they aren't just games to me, they're life lessons, teachings in discipline, the beauty of teamwork, and the raw grit of resilience.

Whether I was shootin' hoops, making touchdowns, or swinging for the fences, each sport whispered its own lessons, crafted its own story. If you have played, then you know what I'm talking about.

The discipline it takes to show up every day, practice after practice, pushing past fatigue, pushing past doubt. The unspoken bond of a team, moving as one, lifting each other, having each other's back, striving for that common goal. And the resilience to get knocked down seven times and stand up eight. To face defeat and say, "Not today!"

See, I'm not just talking about catching balls and scoring touchdowns. I'm talking about the soul-deep lessons these sports gifted me. Lessons I carried with me long after the whistle blew, lessons that made me the man I am today.

So, strap in, folks. In this chapter, we're diving deep into the heart of the field, exploring the power of sport, and how it became my North Star in the midst of my chaos. Let's run this play!

Let me take y'all back, way back. Picture a young me, runnin' around the neighborhood, football in hand, with my crew—just livin', and vibin'. Do you feel me? Now, in the midst of the everyday street scrimmages and pick-up games, a figure steps onto our field. Vincent Straghn was his name. That man had an eye for talent, I'll give him that. He saw something in me, in the midst of our makeshift touchdowns and fumbles. Saw something raw, something real.

Vincent didn't just see a bunch of kids playin' around, he saw potential. So, he pulled a few of us aside, me included. He said he wanted to introduce us to another game— baseball. He was talkin' about a legit team and a league, the Delray

Americans. We were all from Boynton Beach, the next-door neighbor of Delray Beach, so we didn't mind going to Delray to play sports. It was with Mr. Straghn's push that I found myself swingin' a bat, feelin' the weight of a baseball in my hand.

From the age of nine to about twelve, I took to the diamond. Started off in the outfield, the grass under my feet, watching balls soar. But as the years rolled on, as my confidence grew, I wasn't just a jitterbug in the outfield anymore. Hell, by the third year, I was pitching fire and knocking an average of two home runs every damn game. I felt like I was on top of the world. But then, high school hit, and shit changed. You know how it is. The scene shifted.

Baseball wasn't the "in" thing anymore. I mean, look at the stands—hardly a face from the block cheering you on. The diamond was filled with white boys, and my brothers, they were on the basketball court or the gridiron. Baseball started feeling like a distant cousin. It just lost its shine, lost its pull. It wasn't the sport with the swagger. With everyone hyping up football and basketball, the choice for me was clear. It was time to swap the bat for a football.

Let me break it down for y'all. See, in those days, I believe I had more game in baseball than football, truth be told. But football, man, it had the shine, the allure, that street cred. While my skills might've been sharper on the diamond, the pull of the gridiron, the popularity, and the rep it gave you, it was hard to resist.

Now, speaking on challenges, let me paint a picture for you. In the world of baseball, being a southpaw, a leftie, that's a whole different ballgame. And back then, mama's purse wasn't exactly bursting. So, what's my point? I didn't have the luxury of a left-handed glove. Instead, I was out there trying to navigate the game with a right-handed glove. Imagine that shit.

I would field the ball, quickly slip off the glove and toss the ball. It was like dancing backwards in high heels. But the heart wants what the heart wants, and my heart was all in. No challenge was big enough to break a commitment I made to myself. So, I soldiered on, making do with what I had.

Flash forward to the next season and things began to look up. We had another leftie on the squad. So, when he was warming the bench, his glove was mine. But when both of us took the field, well, back to square one with the righthanded glove. Despite all that mess, ya boy made the All-Star team. If that ain't discipline, I don't know what is.

Every day, come hell or high water, I'd be at the spot, waiting for Coach to scoop us up. Mama didn't have wheels, so hitching a ride with Coach was the game plan. Rain, shine, sleet, or storm, I was there. Ready. Waiting. Every damn practice, every damn game. It would've been easy to throw in the towel, to say "Nah, this ain't for me," especially with the cards stacked against me. But that just wasn't my style. I stayed true, rode it out, and gave it everything. That's what you do when you're committed. When you're all in.

Sports is more than scoring points or taking home trophies. It's deeper than that. It's a masterclass in life. It teaches you that everyone, from the star player to the dude fetching water, has a role to play. Everyone's gotta bring something to the table. Everybody's gotta chip in.

See, every person on the team is a cog in the machine. If one cog's rusty or out of place, the whole thing grinds to a halt. Whether you're the young blood rushing water to thirsty players or the quarterback calling the plays, your role matters. It's essential. And understanding your role is half the battle.

Once you understand, you gotta own it, embrace it, and give it your all. When everyone steps up, doing their bit, that's when magic happens. That's when you see the synergy, the unity, and man, that's when you truly win.

And here's another gem. Just like in life, not everyone's cut out for every role. And that's okay. It's crucial to recognize who fits where, and sometimes adjustments need to be made. Maybe someone's got more hustle for the defense or maybe someone's more of a strategist. Placing the right people in the right positions is a game-changer, both on and off the field.

I took that wisdom from the playing field and carried it with me in life, in business, in everything. Recognizing strengths, maximizing potential, and ensuring everyone's pulling their weight. That's what sports drilled into me. And let me tell you, it's made all the difference. It's deeper than just a game, it's life lessons, man. That's the reality.

You see, life is gonna throw some curveballs. But if sports taught me one thing, it's to stand firm and swing back, no matter how tough the pitch.

Let me break this down for you. I'll focus on my journey with the Boynton Beach Bulldogs, another youth sports team that I played with. Our first year of the football program was nothing short of an uphill climb. You see, our city had not had a youth football team in years. Therefore, many players from Boynton played football for the Delray Rocks.

A band of players from Boynton had shifted loyalties to continue to play for Delray Beach. Our team, Boynton Beach Bulldogs were like the leftovers. Our numbers were thin. Our gear was scraps from what our local high school had left behind. Hand-me-down jerseys that had seen better days and equipment that felt like it was from a different era. But here's the thing, it wasn't about what we didn't have, it was about the heart. And damn, did we have heart!

We might've been small in numbers, but man, we were fierce. We went into each game with everything we had, proving that passion can fill the gaps where resources can't. It was that burning dedication that carried us, even when the odds seemed stacked. As time went on, yeah, things got better. Money came in, gear got upgraded. But the fire never dimmed.

1994 was the second year for the Boynton Beach Bulldogs program and by now our team was a little more advanced and experienced. We were ready to take on any team that came our way. We only lost a few games and we advanced to the playoffs.

The first playoff game was against the North Dade Bulldogs. During weigh-in, we did a little trash talking to intensify the game. Bulldog vs. Bulldog and we, the Boynton Beach Bulldogs walked away with the victory. We advanced to the second-round playoff game and then to the third round. This third-round game was not just another playoff game. It was the game right before the Superbowl. We were playing the undefeated Delray Rocks.

The Boynton Beach Bulldogs and the Delray Rocks has always been a great rivalry game since there was always so much at stake.

The week leading up to the game was very tense. And the game was one of the best Boynton vs Delray football games in our history. It was so many people at the game, it was crazy. Folks on the sideline betting serious cash on the game. The Rocks were expected to blow us out because they had an undefeated season and a very good team. Ironically, many of their good players were from Boynton.

At halftime, the score was zero to zero. Yes, as good as the Rocks were, they were unable to score in the first half of the game. Fortunately for them and unfortunately for us, the Rocks played a better second half and we ended up losing the game. For us, a second-year team, it was a victory. Especially when you consider the success we experienced during the season and only being a second-year team. We never gave up and we stood tall until the end.

Then there's my senior year in high school. I'd been waiting to get on the football field, to show them all what I had. I had only played youth football previously. But life's got a funny way of testing you. Just before the season kicked off, I injured my shoulder badly in practice. An injury I endured the entire season. Every tackle felt like a knife twisting in my shoulder, like fire running down my arm. But I gritted my teeth, masked the pain, and got my back in the game, time after time. Even with a chipped bone screaming at me, I couldn't let my team down. Couldn't let myself down.

That year, it wasn't just about the game, it was about proving to myself that no matter the setback, no matter the hurdle, I had the spirit to keep pushing. And that right there; that's life's playbook. No matter how rough the tackle, you pick yourself up, dust off, and charge headfirst into the next play.

Now let's talk about that damn high school football game of Santaluces High playing against one of our rivals, Palm Beach Lakes High. We were both giants on the field, sporting unbeaten records. Six wins, no losses, our egos as inflated as the balls we played with. I juggled roles, wide receiver, cornerback, and improbably, the team's best kicker. I considered myself a true athlete and could play any skilled position. Now, I am not a professional kicker, I just had the knack for it.

The game was neck and neck. We were so close you could taste the victory. And then it fell to me. That pressure -packed moment where one kick could decide it all. The snap, the hold, and... I missed it. 13-14. We lost by the width of a damn goalpost. The blame rained down on me like a Florida thunderstorm. But I held my head up.

Sure, I wasn't born with a kicker's boot, but I was the best shot we had. The coaches, the crowd, the team, they were all pissed. But adversity? That's just another opponent. I buckled down, took the heat, and soldiered on for the rest of the season.

Life, much like the fiercest games, is unpredictable. Just when you think you've got your footing, it has a way of throwing a damn curveball, testing the mettle you're made of.

During that tumultuous senior year, I had another kind of game to play—fatherhood. The whistles and cheers of the field echoed with the beeps of a hospital monitor. As I hustled between practice, school, and hospital corridors, the weight of the new responsibility weighed heavy.

While my teammates worried about the next game, I was facing the vast expanse of parenthood. My newborn son lay in the hospital, and between sport plays and classes, my thoughts were with him. The bleary-eyed nights at his bedside, the early morning drills—I lived a double life, both demanding, both teaching me resilience I never knew I had.

Through all of this, sports became more than just games to me. It was a masterclass in life. Discipline wasn't just about running drills, it was about showing up, even when the world seemed to crumble. I learned the raw value of teamwork, where every player, no matter their role, has their moment to shine or falter.

To be tenacious, to push through even when every fiber of your being wants to tap out. It taught me the weight of a mistake, the price it exacts, and the relentless pursuit of minimizing them. Perfecting your craft, owning your errors, and always, always pushing forward. Those lessons aren't just for the field. They're my playbook for life – in business, in fatherhood, in everything. Always look forward, and if you fall, always fall forward, never back. That's the game.

Beyond the roaring crowds and frenzied pace of the games, sports introduced me to some of life's most enduring lessons. Teams are bound together by an underlying fabric of camaraderie, woven together intricately. Sports became my compass, directing me to those who stood by my side not just in the glory of triumph but also during the suffocating grip of adversity. These moments of shared victory and defeat painted a clearer picture of loyalty.

They acted as a magnifying glass, focusing on those genuine souls who'd pull you up after a tough game or an errant play, showcasing the quality and sincerity of the friendships formed in the crucible of competition.

Coaches and mentors, they're the unsung heroes, the guiding lights in this journey. Their wisdom, drawn from roads we've yet to tread, was an invaluable beacon. Their teachings extended far beyond strategies and techniques; they imparted life lessons that would resonate through time. Figures like Vincent Straghn, Bill Tome, Darryl Wilson, Ray Berger, and Edwin Ross weren't just coaches. They were pillars of strength, emblematic of resilience and perseverance.

But not all interactions were haloed in reverence. There was that episode with Coach Byers that I couldn't shake off. The setting: a routine daily practice, me in my casual element, cracking jokes. Coach Byers was the offensive coordinator and he wanted me to play running back. My head wasn't there for the position, so I was on the sideline doing me until the play was called, and I, in my distraction, missed it entirely. Coach Byers, his patience worn thin, gripped my facemask with an anger I hadn't seen before.

The world slowed as his fury met my indignation. My retaliation was verbal and fierce, a fiery torrent of words echoing my frustration and determination. The helmet, the emblem of my commitment, found itself discarded on the grass as I made for the locker room, fuming. But even in that heated moment, the bonds forged on that field held. My teammates rallied, their words urging reconsideration.

After a strained conversation, Coach Byers and I reached a tenuous understanding. Beyond the strategies and plays, I learned about boundaries, respect, and the fiery passion that can flare when two strong-willed individuals clash.

Man, let me tell y'all something. When you're surrounded by brothers who've walked the same streets, faced the same struggles, and shared the same dreams, there's this bond that's just different.

We've all been there, huddled together on the field, sweat drippin' down our brows, eyes lockin' with that unspoken understanding. We're not just teammates, we're family. We're from the same hood, speakin' the same language. We lift each other up, always keeping that hope alive.

"Man, we got this! We're headed straight to the NFL!" Every day, every practice, pushing one another harder, dreamin' bigger.

But damn, life has a way of switchin' up on you. As the years roll on, those big dreams start to feel distant, like they're getting lost in the rearview. Reality hits hard, you know. And while most of us come to grips with it, some brothers can't let go.

I've got this one homie who is still lacing up his cleats, talking about, "I'm gonna get that call-up any day now." Every time I see him, I'm torn between admiration and wanting to shout, "Bro, are you for real? Time to hang 'em up!" But who am I to kill a man's dream?

We've all been there, chasin' that glimmer, that slim chance. And maybe, just maybe, that's what keeps us alive, keeps us pushin' through the grind. It's that heartbeat of hope, no matter how faint.

But if I were to distill my sports journey, a few lessons would emerge, towering over the rest. There is the iron-willed discipline sports instills, the undying spirit of resilience, the unyielding commitment it demands, and the symbiotic relationship between hard work and its eventual payoff. Every drop of sweat, every strained muscle, it's all a testament to your part in a bigger picture, a grander play.

That's a lesson for life.

At the end of the day, it's not just about the touchdowns, the wins, or even the dreams of the big leagues. It's deeper than that. It's about brotherhood, community, and the heart that beats in all of us. It's the moments when we lift each other up, the laughter after a hard day's practice, and the wisdom shared on those long bus rides home.

The field ain't just grass and dirt, it's a place where dreams are sown, bonds are forged, and life lessons are learned. We've all had our highs and lows, faced our realities, and kept pushing, because when one dream fades, another one rises.

That's the spirit of the game. That's the soul of our journey. As we close this chapter, remember, it's not about where you start or where you end up, but who you become along the way. And let me tell you, the journey is worth every damn step.

Chapter Six
High School Daze

Chillin' in the soft light of my space, my mind drifts back to the days of high school, those pivotal moments that shaped the man I am today. I'm not just reminiscing, this is a deep dive into a torrent of feelings, passions, slip-ups, and life lessons. Echoes of laughter, the sting of heartbreak, the rush of young love, and the sharp edges of rivalry. These aren't just old stories, they're the very threads that weave the fabric of who I am.

The school hallways weren't just routes to classrooms, they were the battlegrounds where battles of identity, ambition, love, and self-discovery unfolded. Imagine the burden of being the pioneer, the first in my lineage to rock that cap, to strut across the graduation stage, basking in the applause. My folks looked on with a mix of surprise, admiration, and hope, witnessing a revolution they never thought possible. The adoration was more than pride, it was an anchor, grounding me and, ironically, driving me forward.

Don't get it twisted. High school wasn't just about acing tests or writing papers. It was a symphony of experiences, a blend of highs and lows, where each note, harmonious or dissonant, shaped the melody of my youth. Through my story, I'll take you on a journey into a transformative period where a hustle-driven boy morphed into a determined young man, aware of his essence and his purpose. So, kick back and travel with me through my high school years where memories, raw and glowing, blend to form the essence of my spirit.

Life in the Santaluces High corridors weren't all sunshine and roses. My juvenile probation was a constant shadow, a harsh reminder of paths I swore never to take again. But even in life's darkest hours, rays of hope often break through. One such ray was my son. His arrival was a wake-up call to responsibility, a call to embrace a promising future.

As a teen wrestling with identity and destiny, sports were my sanctuary. The adrenaline rush, the brotherhood, the grit, and the strategy. It was more than a game; it was a metaphor for life's rollercoaster ride. We had our wild moments as well. Whether we were placing sideline bets or cracking up over an inside joke. These were the vibrant strokes painting the canvas of my high school saga.

And let's not sidestep the academics. Prior to my son's birth, I'll be honest, I was coasting. Doing just enough to fly under the radar. But the birth of a child has a way of resetting one's focus. Recognition started coming in, and suddenly, the trips to the principal's office weren't about the mischief but about the milestones. With each affirmation, I felt empowered, trading my reputation as a troublemaker for one of potential and promise.

It was during these transformative years that I embraced dreadlocks. They were more than a trend, they were a statement, an affirmation of authenticity and identity. If you weren't a true Rasta/ Jamaican Dred, having locks took on a different meaning. While famous folks

might have been rocking dreadlocks, in my world, they represented a lived experience. Despite whispers of backlash, especially in the sports realm, I stood firm, unwavering in my pledge of self-expression.

The same held true for gold teeth. In my mind and among many of my peers, gold teeth weren't just accessories, they were symbols of success, of having 'made it'.

At the high school level, these symbols—the dreadlocks, the blinging gold teeth, the athletic prowess, and my blossoming intellectual acumen were more than mere choices. They were badges of honor, representing my struggles, dreams, and an unyielding will to rise above.

High school was a whirlwind. And in that whirlwind, humor was my anchor. The booming laughter, the razor-sharp wit, the camaraderie, they made the hallways pulse with life. The stakes were high, and not just in the classroom. The gambling was a thrill. Dice games in hidden corners, playing cards in the cafeteria and classrooms. But these weren't just games, they were all about the hustle. Tonk, Blackjack, Spades, these card games were a rite of passage. Did I mention we played for money? The stakes made everything more exciting.

Then there were the sub days! Discovering a substitute teacher was our instructor for the day was like striking gold. We'd quickly learn which students were absent that day and assume their identity for a few hours. Today, I'm John Walker, I'd say, ready to weave a whole persona for kicks. Whether it was flipping garbage cans, holding an impromptu card game on someone's desk, or just being a pain in the ass, substitute teachers gave us that bit of room to be rebellious and playful.

Our network didn't include smartphones like today. It would be a whisper in the hallway, a nod across the cafeteria, and we'd converge on the chosen classroom, ready for action.

Then, there were the ladies! The ladies with their charm and mystery brought layers of complexity to an already intricate web of experiences.

Girls had a soft spot for the jokers, hustlers, and cool dudes like myself.

Being blessed with good looks and swag can be a blessing and a curse at the same time which can lead to a little trouble here and there.

This one young lady who had a huge crush on me invited me to her home. Her father happened to be a Boynton Beach police officer who did not like me. So, there we were, in her room, about to get it on. I mean naked, kissing and then we heard the keys turning the doorknob to the front door. It's her dad, in uniform and on duty, no less.

She quickly directed me to the closet to hide. Her dad burst into the room, demanding to know why she was in her room while the television was on in the living room. Then, he headed straight for the closet. There I am, caught red-handed, standing there with nothing on but my regrets. All I could muster was "sorry, sir", not that it helped. He gritted his teeth and pulled out his baton. He then punched me in my mouth, and I began to bleed. I was dazed but I managed to make it out of the house alive.

I ran to the next-door neighbor's house, who was a nice lady that bandaged me up. Then I see the girl, running out, crying, saying she's calling the cops. And I'm like, "Your dad is the police!"

After that, her dad was out on the streets, making threats against my life. That guy truly despised me, and I did everything I could to steer clear of him. That was a crazy situation and I thank God that it did not end differently.

When you are "that dude," these are the type of situations you can easily find yourself involved in. The ladies really had it for me, and I was the crush of many girls in high school.

But there was one who stood out, a force of nature with a spark in her eyes, and she was mine. With her by my side, I felt invincible during those times. It was because of my relationship with her that I began to change how I was livin' and who I was hangin' with. In her shadow, I became untouchable, all while cracking jokes and living life on my terms.

Now, if you ever ask me about my most precious moments at school, I'd start with lunchtime. My favorite was the fish with the mac & cheese combo. Those mad dashes to the cafeteria were competitive. It was like the cafeteria Olympics. Any girl that wanted to maintain her "cute" demeanor, well, that went out the window really quick. Soon as that bell went off, it was a mad dash. Every single day, without fail, it looked like we were gearing up for a 100 -meter dash, heels, fresh kicks, and all.

However, on a serious note, if I had to choose an academic class that truly struck a chord, it'd be History. What I love so much about history is it allows you to look back and reflect on how things once were. There's something captivating about understanding our roots, about piecing together stories from the past. Learning about battles, evolving cultures, and civilizations that thrived and fell. History gives perspectives and reminds us that we are just a small part of a vast, intricate interconnected system of the human experience. The more you understand the past, you can appreciate the present and look forward to a brighter future.

Another class that I connected well with was *Communities in School.* It was an eye-opener. Yeah, it was designed for students like me—folks who, based on statistics and backgrounds, were labeled "at-risk" of dropping out. But man, that class was so much more than what its label suggested. It was a safe haven, a space where we delved into real life stuff. We discussed our dreams, mapped out goals, learned about the importance of good credit, things that genuinely mattered outside the school walls.

Every *Communities in School* class felt like a therapy session. I was able to voice thoughts and concerns that I might not have otherwise expressed. It was laid back yet impactful, and credit goes to our teacher, Coach Klammer.

Under his guidance, the class wasn't just about checking boxes on a curriculum, it was about understanding life. Through those discussions, I directed my passion, which was and is a desire to uplift others, and give back to the community that raised me.

Beyond academic challenges, it was a journey into life's complex web, a class where dreams were born, and futures were shaped. Stepping into Santaluces, I felt an unwavering conviction that I would graduate with a high school diploma.

It was a promise that I had made to myself. Against all odds, against all scorn, I was determined to walk that stage. It might've seemed like a pipe dream, especially considering the missteps of my youth. But every stumble, every slip-up only strengthened my determination. I was a high school student, and I was gonna make it!

High school wasn't all about books and grades though. There were parties, girls, of course, football and basketball games, and the hustle. These moments in time should never be forgotten.

While most teenagers at sixteen are looking to borrow their parent's car or grab the bus, I was out there wheeling and dealing automobiles. No longer stealing them, I was making real money moves.

By the end of my junior year, I had bought and flipped five cars! Man, I even bought a ride for my girl. How crazy is that? A young kid whose family didn't own a car, much less a driver's license, and yet I was navigating the world of cars like a seasoned dealer.

My car of choice, might you ask, was good ole Chevys. The very first car I purchased was a lime green Chevy Impala that I bought from my friend, J-Red. It wasn't just about the car; it was about what it represented. In my hood, your car was an extension of your identity. A nice, wet paint job, shiny big rims, rumbling engine, and some thump in the trunk – these were symbols of success, of status. It was the culture, the unspoken language of the streets.

Now, here I am today, reflecting on the past. What I survived during those four years is etched in my memory. I often revisit those memories, the good and the bad. It's funny how so much can happen in such a short amount of time.

But it was those experiences that made me who I am today. I may not have left with perfect grades, but I did leave with lessons more valuable than gold medals. I learned that you never give up on yourself. I learned to take every opportunity given. And don't ever forget to have fun. Those lessons I carry with me, forever etched in my heart. High school may be over, but the legacy of Santaluces will remain.

The world is ever-changing and as I continue forward on this journey through life, no matter where it takes me, I promise you one thing: I will never forget the lessons of my past. Those memories are part of me, and no matter how far away I travel, they will continue to shape who I am for years to come.

High school was an incredible experience that provided me with a unique perspective on life. It gave me the opportunity to learn from my peers and understand that in life, there are no guarantees, there will always be highs and lows. But it's during those times that we grow the most and take away powerful lessons. Lessons that I still carry with me as I continue to navigate this world.

From the classrooms to the paths of life, my experiences have served as a foundation for growth. The memories remain vivid, but the lessons are for a lifetime. I'm thankful for the days spent in high school, and all the experiences that came with it. They will stay with me forever, always reminding me of who I am and who I strive to become.

PART THREE
Dreaming & Doing

Chapter Seven
College Life:
A Fresh Perspective

"My mind was in a constant state of expansion."

When I think back to my days at Bethune Cookman College, now known as Bethune Cookman University, a wave of nostalgia mixed with gratitude sweeps over me.

Let me paint a picture for you. Visualize a young, eager Black man stepping into this historically rich campus, hungry for knowledge and thirsty for new experiences. College wasn't just the next step after high school, it was a monumental leap into a world of possibilities, a realm where the horizons of my understanding stretched far beyond what I had ever imagined.

As I prepared to make my move and take my talents to the destination known for having the World's Most Famous Beach, Daytona Beach, Florida, I did so, driving my navy blue Cadillac with a digital dashboard and leather seats filled with my belongings.

I said I was a Chevy man, but I knew I would be doing a lot of driving up and down I-95 from Daytona Beach to South Florida, so I wanted something more dependable, and Cadillacs were known to be good cars on the highway. It was fresh!

I packed my car with all my belongings including everything the college asked students to bring. I had all my life packed up in that Cadillac, including a chest I still have to this day.

I packed an ironing board, sheets, blankets, etc. Once I was packed up, I made my rounds to say my goodbyes. I had to double back to see my son and girlfriend for more hugs and kisses. Then I hit the road.

Back in the day, there was no Siri telling you to "Turn left in 300 feet." Instead, I printed out a Google map to help me navigate to Daytona Beach. I'd been to Daytona before for the Spring Bling and Black College Reunion but still, I needed the map because I didn't want to make a wrong turn. Exit 67, man, I remember it like yesterday.

Now, I won't front, when I first set foot on campus, it felt like home. However, I arrived knowing my purpose and I was focused. BCC, as we fondly called it, wasn't just about hitting those books, of course, there was a lot of that. BCC was also a sacred ground of self-discovery.

The intellectual growth was phenomenal. I was introduced to thinkers and ideologies that challenged every pre-conceived notion I held. There were late-night debates in the dorm rooms and enlightening lectures that left my head spinning. My mind was in a constant state of expansion.

Then there was the newfound independence. I was my own man, making decisions, both good and... let's just say, learning experiences. This freedom wasn't just about parties or setting my own bedtime. It was deeper. It was about defining who I was, without the confines or labels of my past.

But BCC wasn't just an institution, it was a community, a family. It was a place where defining moments were crafted, where friendships were solidified, and where life lessons, both inside and outside the classroom, took root. Every corner of that campus, every brick, every tree, holds a memory, a lesson, a piece of my journey from a boy to a man.

So, pull up a chair, get comfortable, and journey with me as I navigate you through those golden years. The laughter, the struggles, the triumphs, and the missteps – it's all here. Welcome to my college life at Bethune Cookman, a fresh perspective on a transformative era that shaped the man I am today.

The importance of education was something I grasped early on. It wasn't just about book smarts; it was the ticket to better opportunities and a broader horizon. Growing up, it was always hammered into us: "Get that high school diploma at the very least." That sentiment echoed in my head and pushed me to earn mine.

Football and sports started whispering dreams of college into my ear. There was a moment when the idea of joining the Marines took hold of my mind, the allure of the uniform and the honor of service. But a chat with an Army recruiter made me doubt my eligibility – rumors had it that my past mistakes, particularly a sale of cocaine, a felony, might be a barrier. I had already been led to believe that certain wrongs in my record could lock you out of the military, so I wasn't shocked. But hey, whether that was true or not, college soon emerged as the next logical step, especially if sports were involved.

Choosing a college, well, that was another journey. The world was vast, and there were so many institutions calling out. But my son tethered my heart closer to home. Mrs. Maxine Perry-Dupont, a proud alumna of the illustrious Bethune Cookman University (BCU), threw the idea my way. The college was close, just under a three-hour drive. Close enough to be near my son. No one in my family had stepped foot in a college, but I'd heard tales of the college experience – the camaraderie, the fun, and yes, the ladies.

I also had to consider the fact that my juvenile probation was on my back about the restitution I owed. I was still in a re-entry program, facing a decision: a restrictive level 8 program or embrace the freedom of college. The Department of Juvenile Justice made threats of me going back to a program if I did not make my payments.

Because I was doing well in high school, the judge informed me that if I enrolled in college, I wouldn't have to go to the level 8 program and the restitution fees I owed would be waived. Let me tell you, the choice was clear as day. Bethune Cookman was calling, and I answered, stepping onto its campus with a desire to major in sociology.

It was a toss-up between business and sociology for a while. But while I felt I had a good grasp of business, I was driven to understand the intricacies of society, the struggles of my people, and the underpinnings of human behavior.

Why were we trapped in these cycles? How did societal structures affect us? I wanted to dive deep into those questions, and so, my journey at Bethune Cookman began.

Attending an Historically Black College and University (HBCU) is an experience like no other. My experience at the Great Bethune Cookman was an amazing and joyful one. Back in the day, it was always something you had to go through as a newbie. From being on a sports team to being a member of the band, or even just being a student, you were going to go through something.

As a freshman on the yard, you were considered a BCC Crab. You had to declare to the yard "I'm proud to be a BCC Crab" and you would receive your Crab hat. The Crab hat was a loud green colored visor that freshmen had to wear or carry everywhere. If you were a freshman and did not have it, you couldn't get into places like the cafe, class, or college activities. This would go on until homecoming week where you get to stomp on the Crab hat and no longer be a BCC Crab. This was exciting for us Freshmen because it gave us pride and a sense of accomplishment.

Now, freshmen weren't typically allowed to have cars on campus back then, but you know your boy always had some moves, right? I pulled a smooth one on the lady in the Admissions office and got myself a parking pass. I was one of few freshmen rolling with four wheels. But I still wanted the full college experience, so most times, I'd park it and do as the students without cars would do. Every so often I would hop on the shuttle bus or even the Greyhound once, instead of racking up miles on my Caddy. Plus, I wasn't trying to flex too hard.

College life was electric. Everywhere you looked, talent on top of talent. You think you're the funniest guy on the block. Bam! Here's someone funnier. Got moves on the field or the court, there's someone who's been the star player in their hometown. Hell, even with the ladies, the game stepped up. There were queens who were turning heads and breaking necks. The competition was sky-high. Everything was amplified to a higher level, and I was loving it.

I went to Bethune Cookman with the hopes of playing football but the desire for the game slowly became short lived. Looking back, a part of me wishes I took sports more seriously and gave it my all. Because even with minimum effort, I shined. Imagine the possibilities if I'd poured my heart into it. But hey, life's a journey, full of what-ifs and might-have-been. All I know is that my time at Bethune Cookman College molded me, taught me, and gave me memories I'll cherish forever.

Yet, college wasn't without its challenges. My son, a little under a year old at the time, faced health issues. I found myself torn between school and home, but life has its way of working things out. I left Daytona Beach to return home for the second semester of my freshman year. Bethune Cookman had a satellite program in Palm Beach County, so I continued my studies even while being home for the semester.

At the start of my sophomore year, I returned to Daytona energized and filled with hopes and dreams. I sold the Cadillac and purchased a nice blue Chevy Caprice. I updated the sound system to hear the sounds of Eight Ball & MJG, Scarface, JT Money, Trick Daddy, No Limit Soldiers and Cash Money's Hot Boyz on my trips up and down I-95. I had my trunk bangin' to that good music.

My roommates and I decided to rent an off-campus apartment to allow us a little more college freedom because Cookman had rules that were strictly enforced in the dorm. It was time for us to bounce.

My girlfriend and son moved to Daytona a few months later. Having them move to Daytona Beach with me during the second semester of my sophomore year was a gamechanger.

It felt right having them there although they were there only for one year and moved back home.

When I finally locked onto my mission of inspiring folks and adding value to others, it was a moment that hit me hard during my junior year. College life was the shit. If there was a button to rewind time and re-live that phase, best believe I'd smash it without a second thought.

Back in high school, I had that swagger and thought I was too cool to do anything besides sports. I didn't want to be involved in school clubs, Student Government, or anything like that. But college humbled me. It made me understand that if I wanted to take full advantage of this experience, I needed to step it up, do more, and be involved. I realized that the people on the dance floor always have the most fun. So, I dove right in.

I became part of the sociology club, even became the President. I rolled with the Criminal Justice Association. I organized study groups, and even participated in a work study gig that got me some extra cash. College wasn't just a phase, man. It was a whole damn evolution.

Let me share one of the best decisions I made in my life. That decision was to become a member of the Mighty Omicron Epsilon Chapter of Omega Psi Phi Fraternity Inc. during my Junior year at Bethune Cookman College. One of the best damn decisions, hands down!

I remember back in the day at our church, Mrs. Jackson saying to me, "Boy, when you get to college, become a Que." I had no idea what she was talking about when she said it, but when I arrived at college, there they were, the Omegas, the Ques, the Bruhz were doing their thing on campus. These dudes weren't just partying, strolling and hopping on the yard, they were putting in the work, making a positive impact on the campus and in the community. A couple of them were in my classes. They were intelligent movers and shakers; sharp brothers, and I thought, 'Man, I need to get in on this.'

What inspired me to want to be a part of the organization was that I wanted to be a part of something great, something different, something mutually beneficial where a shared value is really shared.

I always noticed, every time I'd flip through a magazine or a book, or even researched a well-known Black person, a lot of the influential black figures were members of Black fraternities and sororities known as the Divine 9.

The Divine Nine is also known as the National Pan-Hellenic Council, a collaborative organization of nine historically African American Greek lettered fraternities and sororities. They were founded with the purpose of enhancing academic and professional opportunities and providing service to the community.

I want you to think about Black movers and shakers you may know. Educators, coaches, doctors, lawyers, judges, athletes, scientists, entertainers, and entrepreneurs. You will find that many of these influential people are a part of the Divine Nine and rock their Greek letters.

Initially, I almost jeopardized my opportunity of becoming a member of Omega Psi Phi Fraternity Inc. It was during my sophomore year, and I got caught up in some silly shit. I was throwing eggs on campus. See, it was Halloween, me and some of the homies was on some clown shit. Different students would dress in all black and throw eggs at each other. Well, school security saw us and began to chase us. I ran into the dorm and jumped in the shower. Security found me and asked me to come out and I was taken to the security office to be written up.

I had to appear before the Men's Senate, a group that governed the male student body. This group served as jurors on disciplinary actions like these and they would hear and decide the fate of my punishment.

I thought I was done for a minute, especially with what I was faced with. When I realized some Omegas were sitting on the panel, I was praying favor would be on my side. Luckily, they saw something in me, and gave a brother a chance. Instead of getting kicked out of school and labeling me with a disciplinary action, they decided I was not guilty.

Blessings, man.

Look here, no shade, but I wasn't really checking for the other frats. I knew from the beginning that I wanted to rock the royal purple and old gold of Omega Psi Phi. I had already envisioned me walking across the yard, rockin' a frat shirt, fatigue shorts and gold boots.

Man, one thing I admired about the brothers of Omega Psi Phi Fraternity Inc. was their versatility. Some dressed fly as hell, others were down-to-earth, but all of them authentic, real, and solid dudes.

I was like, this is where I can be me, no fronts, no airs.

And the parties? Shit, the Ques knew how to throw down! Ain't no party like a Que dawg party cause a Que dawg party don't stop. Good times I tell ya!

The process to become a member of the organization is something that you take seriously, and you keep it on the low. The process was real, and you don't want everyone in your business. It's a journey that shapes you, humbles you and builds you. There were so many lessons learned and sacrifices made during the process. What I admired most about the process is that it challenged you beyond measure, pushed you beyond your limits, and forced you to conquer the impossible.

The journey was long, and it was life changing. It allowed us as a line to truly embrace our cardinal principles of manhood, scholarship, perseverance, and to uplift. The journey created a lifelong bond between six brothers known as *Stealth Mode 6* of the Mighty Omicron Epsilon Chapter.

Shoutout to my line brothers: "Ceasar", Dogmatic, Lumberjack, Gambino, and X-Files. Of course, there's me, Kaotic. We started as seventeen deep but ended as six solid brothers. What an experience. The memories, the lessons, the brotherhood. Wouldn't trade it for the world.

Now don't get me wrong, as a college student, it can be rough, and the struggle is real. That wasn't the case for me, I've been a hustler all my life and making money was what I knew best. My resume was always good on the streets, so I had to do my thang to take care of my responsibilities. I wasn't proud of it, and it wasn't something I glorified.

I was only doing me and staying out of the way as I was focused on my education and my money. I kept it on the low and moved in silence. It helped me do what I had to do for myself and send some cash home to Mom and my girlfriend.

Nevertheless, my college experience was everything. We were located in Daytona Beach, home of the World's Most Famous Beach, and it was lit! We had it all – Daytona 500, Spring Bling, MTV doing their thing every spring. Don't even get me started on Black College Reunion. Bruh, that was the event!

Black College Reunion (BCR) was an opportunity for students that attended HBCUs to come together and have a good time. Folks from across the country would come to Daytona Beach to indulge in the four-day weekend extravaganza. But over time, it lost its essence and focus. Outsiders started showing up, and it wasn't about the students anymore. Kind of muddied the waters, took away from the whole purpose.

I also must tell you that college was a networking goldmine for me. My charisma and determination allowed me to be in a position to get tight with some professors. One even tried setting me up with her daughter! Ha ha! I guess being charming was a blessing and a curse. I also had the reputation as the go-to guy for class notes and study groups. When the professors were teaching lessons, half the time I'm thinking, "Man, I've lived this." So, I was all in, soaking it all up.

I lived for those college football games and the parties. The Florida Classic is the annual game against our number one rival, Florida A & M University and of course Homecoming. And the road trips with my frat brothers to other campuses. Those were the days.

I met some big-time folks – doctors, lawyers, athletes, entrepreneurs, entertainers, and others. Lifelong friends to this day.

Was college a culture shock? Nah, man. College felt like home. It was like being in a village of us, good ole Black folks, with a sprinkle of white folks. We had our beefs here and there with folks from different cities clashing, you know how it is. Then the locals, man, they had some beef with us college kids.

I remember that tragic night with Derell, a student at BCC. It was Spring of 2001, some locals rolled up on campus, started beef with our clic, and just like that, a senseless shooting that ended the life of a student, a good dude from

Palm Beach County, my home. That hit different, and it hurt badly.

But all in all, college taught me a ton of lessons. Leadership, perseverance, and how to keep pushing, no matter what. It was a journey, and I wouldn't trade it for the world.

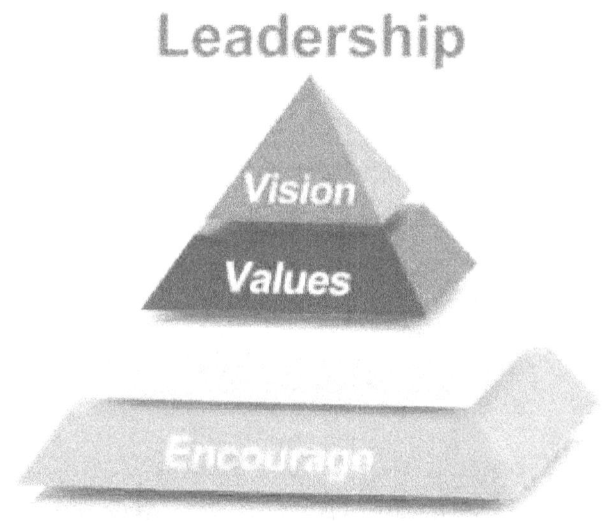

Chapter Eight
The Grind to My Destiny

Let's roll it back to a time when the dream was bigger than the bank account. As a matter of fact, my dream was taller than any skyscraper in a big city. So, as you read this chapter, I want the following thought to stay in front of your mind. *What you do on your 9 to 5 is what's going to keep you afloat, but what you do from 5 to 9 is what's gonna get you to that next level of success.*

See, I wasn't born with a silver spoon in my mouth, but I had that fire in my belly, that undeniable urge to create, innovate, and elevate. My first ventures? Whew! Let's just say not everything glittered like gold. I've tasted failure more than I'd care to admit, but it's the bitter bites that make the sweet success taste so damn good.

I've journeyed from selling shoes out the back of my truck to my first failed startup, to finally hitting it big and knowing what it felt like to see something you've birthed flourish - this journey was a rollercoaster. No cap.

We're about to explore the ups, downs, lefts, rights, and all the wild turns in between. Ready to roll with me on this entrepreneurial ride? Let's get it.

 Let's start at the beginning, where the grind met the ground and where passion collided with real-world challenges. Fresh out of college, I had my degree in hand, and I was on top of the world, right? Wrong. With my gold teeth flashing and limited experience on paper, the job hunt was tougher than I thought. I might have been a star in my own hood, but the workforce scene wasn't quite vibing with me.

One day, out of the blue, I received this letter from my cousin. He's locked up. In the letter, he's telling me about a program he wanted me to check out for him. So, I reached out to the lady he mentioned in the letter. Her name was Mrs. Katherine Burns. She was heading up the program.

Now, when I reached out to her, I kept it real with her. I told her, "Look, I'm not behind bars, but I'm trapped in my own kind of prison. I have a lengthy juvenile record and I believe it is preventing me from landing a job in my field of study."

I had dreams, y'all. I wanted to work with DJJ – the Department of Juvenile Justice. Some folks working for DJJ had pulled me out of some tight spots back in the day when I was messing up. But when it came to giving me a job, doors slammed all because of some charges from way back. I was starting to think differently about DJJ. I thought about all the good things I'd said about DJJ. The transformational stories I shared, and the fact that I was the poster boy success story for DJJ and now, nothing. 'Y'all gonna do me like that?' I thought to myself. I couldn't believe it!

I'm not going to lie, it hit me hard. But every setback is a setup for a comeback. And this was just my beginning. Sitting down and meeting with Mrs. Katherine Burns was the game-changer I never saw coming. After opening up to her about my cousin and my own story, she took a moment, looked me straight in the eyes, and said, "Ricky, you are special. Is it ok if I pray with you?"

"Sure, of course, Mrs. Burns," I answered quickly. She began to pray.

Mrs. Burns was a God-fearing woman and I appreciated that about her. After the prayer, I had this good feeling running through my body. I felt really good. That prayer really touched me and made me realize that I had to switch up the narrative. The streets, the hustle, the shortcuts - it was time to leave all that behind. No more risking everything for quick cash. Things were different now.

Before I felt like I had nothing to lose, and I was willing to take big life risks. But understanding my future and what I wanted out of life, I realized I had too much to lose by involving myself with risky behavioral choices. I had bigger dreams to chase: owning a home, becoming a businessman, serving my community, and being a contributing member of society. I wanted a fair shot at providing a quality lifestyle for me and my family. I understood some changes had to be made for the changes to happen.

Mrs. Burns mentioned that if she had a position available, she would hire me right now. She then went on to tell me that she was working on a huge grant, and she would like me to be a part of it. We discussed my strengths and weaknesses and identified that my limited experience was something I needed to work on, and she would assist me.

"How about volunteering for now," suggested Mrs. Burns, "and let's see where it takes you."

I agreed to volunteer three days a week, from 9am – 2pm. I would go to her office and volunteer my time.

Within three months of volunteering my time, I had learned so much. I tightened up on my computer skills which allowed me to become efficient in Microsoft Word, Excel, and PowerPoint. I learned how to put together resumés and interact with clients. My communication skills elevated to another level, and I gained the confidence to facilitate workshops. I learned so much and the volunteer opportunity helped me understand how important it was to always be ready when opportunity knocks.

Then one day out of nowhere, Mrs. Burns invited me into her office and informed me that a temporary position had become available, and I was the perfect fit. It was unbelievable. All I could do was fall to my knees and thank God.

It was a program called *Probationers Educational Growth (P.E.G.)*. They were working wonders with folks on probation, sharpening their skills for the real world, resumé writing, interview prep, the works.

Volunteering for the program, and absorbing knowledge like a sponge really paid off. And now, this was my big break, working for the P.E.G. Program. I was providing guidance to individuals on probation. I was helping with their job search, and I was passing on everything I'd learned. I was making a huge impact on folks' lives, helping them reach their ultimate goal of obtaining gainful employment. I was very passionate about the work because of my personal experience, and I understood their struggle.

As I got deeper into the work, Mrs. Burns dropped a hint about the big grant she was working on. She made it clear that if the grant came through, she had a permanent position for me.

Just when I thought I was settled, the program wrapped up a year later. Mrs. Burns was still at it, chasing the grant, and promising another opportunity. Meanwhile, I was back on the job hunt. I applied for a position at Children's Home Society (CHS) as a coordinator for a mentoring program. The position involved matching mentors with children that had a parent incarcerated. Because of my experience working with probationers, I was a great fit and they offered me the job. Just when I was celebrating my new role, guess who rings? Mrs.

Burns. The grant had finally come through and she wanted me on board.

Here's where things took an unexpected turn. I was offered a new position that paid double what I would earn at CHS. Yet, I believed in honoring commitments. I explained to Mrs. Burns that I had accepted a position with CHS, and I did not want to renege on the position. She surprised me with a proposal for part-time work. It was a perfect solution, and I accepted the role as a case manager. Balancing two jobs was intense, but the hustle was exhilarating, and the rewards were immensely satisfying. I always had more than one job since that day.

At Children's Home Society, I was totally committed to my position as the Volunteer Coordinator. This role was not just a job, instead it was a chance to make a real difference, and it taught me so much.

On the other hand, my part-time role was with Workforce Alliance and the Department of Corrections, with a program called SAVORI, short for Serious Violent Offender Re-Entry Initiative. My task was daunting yet fulfilling – working with hardcore offenders returning to Palm Beach County. My days were spent traveling across Florida, visiting various prisons, and helping those individuals plan for a life outside. I assisted in finding them housing and employment to reduce the risk of re-offending.

It's incredible to think that I went from desperately seeking a single job to expertly handling multiple roles. And it wasn't just about the money, it was about the positive impact I was making on the lives of others.

This opportunity was the perfect assist, setting me up to score my first home. I was doing what was needed to reach my goal of purchasing a home. Working, saving money consistently and taking care of business.

Fast forward, and after five years, the grant-funded role ended, but I continued to work my full-time position at CHS. My journey then led me to the Beacon Center, where I supervised support programs and afterschool initiatives, eventually being promoted to director. After five fulfilling years, I felt established, yet my dream of venturing into real estate lingered.

Remember the golden smile I mentioned earlier? My mouth shined bright with gold teeth. I fantasized about getting involved in real estate and did not want to be judged or not taken seriously based upon my appearance. We live in a world where 50% of the people will accept you just the way you are and the other 50% won't. The problem for me was you never know which 50% of the audience you are in front of and when it comes to my money, their judgement wasn't going to be an option. So, in 2008, I had my gold teeth removed. It was another great decision I made.

After the Beacon Center, I transitioned to the Bridges program, and after several years there, I joined the Pathways to Prosperity family to lead the Healthier Boynton Beach initiative. This marked a shift towards community engagement and resident focused work, improving the overall health with a focus on caregivers, mental health, healthy eating, etc. Our end game was creating a culture of healthy habits to improve health outcomes in our community.

The interview process this time around was different. I wasn't there to prove myself. It seemed as if they needed a person like me more than I needed the job. I was from the community, well connected and had the ability to influence others. These were valuable attributes they felt were needed for the position and I had them all and some. They had a vision, and I was a key part of it.

Now, here's the cherry on top. During the mist of my career advancement, I snagged my mortgage broker's license in 2007 and my real estate license in 2008. No big deal, just another dream turned reality. Stick around, and I'll tell you how that went down. Jumping into real estate is just another chapter in my mad adventure.

Now, it's not news that hustling is second nature to me. From cutting grass, cleaning yards, to selling newspaper subscriptions, oranges, mangoes, candy, shoes, and even drugs, if there was money to be made, I made it. But before we get into the real estate dealings, let me slide back a bit to 2003.

I had dipped my toes in the music biz. Yeah, you heard right. I started a record label with my homie, J-Red. The two of us went way back and he was an ace rapper from our school days. We both had the hustle spirit, so we thought we could possibly spin some tunes together.

Although I'm a hustler by nature, I had no knowledge of the music industry. I knew that if I wanted to invest my time and money in this game, I needed to educate myself on the inner workings of the game. So, I took $2,500 and educated myself on the ins and outs of the record label business. No joke. I took a business class, focusing on how to run a record label and become an A & R representative. I learned the business and how to find promising new artists.

That's when the music game truly took off.

The business class was a game-changer for me, especially when it came to running my record label. I picked up some killer insights on how to manage finances and market the heck out of my artists. It's all about strategy. But it wasn't just about the music biz, those skills translated really well into my other ventures. I was understanding customer needs and how to make my brand pop, that was gold. And I got way sharper at negotiating deals.

It's like, once you grasp the nuts and bolts of running one business, applying that knowledge to another just flows naturally. So, yeah, that class wasn't just schoolwork, it laid down the blueprint for how I handle all my businesses now.

Music has been in my veins since I was a child. And my homie, J Red, well he could spit bars from gangsta rap to grown-up beats. This dude was a beast when it came to music.

He was a true lyricist with so much creative talent. To this day he is one of the best from Palm Beach County.

So, let me share with you how it all went down. One day, we were just chillin' and choppin' it up. 'Why not start our own label?' we thought. I had the business mind and skills, and J Red had the lyrical skills, and he had a taste of the industry with a few labels, but he wanted his own.

We brainstormed, threw around some names, and landed on S.M.O.B. Records. Fancy, right? It stood for 'Superior Men of Business.' We weren't just making noise; we were making statements.

Through S.M.O.B., I met the very talented Ontario "OJ" Johnson and Chantelle Brown. Soon, we became the talk of the town. S.M.O.B. was the name on everyone's lips. If only the artists had stayed on the mic and out of jail, I swear, we could've been the next big thing.

Picture us producing *Cash Money* vibes in Boynton Beach, Palm Beach County. We were hustling, selling CDs right out of the trunk, building connections with all the local corner stores and barbershops.

Every week, I'd swing by, drop off the CDs, pick up the cash. I negotiated 80/20 distribution and consignment deals with the local corner stores and barbershops that agreed to work with us. They received 20% or $2.00 for each $10.00 CD sold.

I've always been a businessman, so the art of negotiating came easy to me. I even negotiated deals with local clubs and events. J-Red loved performing and he would set the stage on fire. When my boy hit the stage, he would bring the whole city out. Boynton would always show up deep to support!

All this was going down in my post-college, early twenties days. As I continued my life journey, figuring out this thing we call life, I had to understand what was important to me and my future. It was a lot coming my way and I needed to have a plan. Before diving in any deeper with S.M.O.B., I had a sit-down with myself, figuring out what I wanted. It wasn't about fame or the Benjamins. It was about the hustle, the grind, the learning. I wanted to hone my business skills, including my negotiating tactics, all aspects of business.

J Red, the artist, was an absolute local legend. His tracks still got folks in Boynton rocking S.M.O.B. ink. We had other artists, like D-Moe and Quissha, all had mad skills. But life, it threw its curveballs. J Red kept getting entangled with the law, and it reached a point where I had to step back. I gave him my blessings, but the label scene was becoming too messy for me.

Kickstarting the record company was a learning experience. I viewed the entire ride as a treasure trove of lessons. Each step, each hiccup was like school. I'd always catch myself pondering, 'What's the real goal here? The bucks or the brains?' And for me, it was always about the wisdom and man, did I learn a lot with that label. I'm talking trust, being straight-up, making deals, playing the negotiation game, all that jazz.

Sure, I faced some real curveballs, but each one sharpened my business game. From beats to boardrooms, every stumble turned me into a sharper entrepreneur.

In the beginning of my entrepreneurial game, I had this itch, right? I wanted to learn more about business and how to start my own business, so I took an entrepreneur class. The class lasted eight weeks, and I learned the importance of starting an LLC and S-Corporation and the benefits that came along with it. I learned about marketing a business and how to put together a business plan.

So, as S.M.O.B.'s beat began to fade, my entrepreneurial spirit turned up the volume. I felt the allure of real estate, so I created Petty Investments. And that, my friends, is the saga of my tunes and tales.

So now, real estate had my full attention and I decided that my own investment company was the business move to make and Petty Investments was not only birthed into existence, it is still up and running.

At first, I'll be honest, it was just a name. I wasn't even sure about the whole thing. I did put together a bum ass business plan focused on buying properties in college towns and renting them to college students. I didn't have the cash for the business to take off at the time, but the bug to start a business was strong.

I was wearing multiple hats, not just the real estate hat. Remember P.E.G., where Ms. Burns took me under her wing? Well, I flipped that knowledge into workshops. I taught the youth about business, how to interview for jobs, writing resumes and budgeting, that was my thing. I worked with after school programs. I'd charge a nominal fee. It was all under the umbrella of Petty Investments. It was another hustle and another opportunity to make money and save money to support my dream. I'm always on the lookout for new ideas and business opportunities.

Here's another example. A good buddy of mine from college, who ran a mobile phone store, kept telling me about the financial potential. I mulled it over for a while, considering I already had my plate full. But once I decided to jump into the mobile phone store game, I started doing my homework to understand the ins and outs of the business. It quickly became clear that I needed a business partner to help carry the load.

So, I reached out to my boy OJ and laid out the opportunity. He was all in. We got together, hashed out the details, and agreed to dive in together. We decided on the name R&O Wireless and found a prime location in a busy plaza.

I negotiated a sweet deal with the realtor for the space. But OJ and I knew the importance of a solid business plan, so we agreed to get one prepared professionally. I contacted someone I thought I knew well, a real business guru, the instructor for the entrepreneurship class I had previously taken. This person helped me start my first business, so I had confidence in them. This person was sharp and well connected – just what we needed.

When I told the person about our idea, they agreed to draft a business plan for a steep $3600 fee. I discussed it with OJ, and despite the cost, we agreed to have the business plan completed since we trusted the person's expertise.

I put down a $1800 deposit and waited for the draft. Two weeks later, the plan arrived in my inbox. I skimmed through it and paid the remaining $1800 balance. But then, OJ called me up. He asked me if I had read the business plan.

When I reviewed the plan in more detail, I noticed something funny. The preparer had mistakenly left a business name in the plan that I happened to Google and it's the exact same business plan she gave us, word for word! Turns out, the plan was a straight copy-paste job from another business, just with our name slapped on it. We paid $3600 for a plagiarized plan!

I was livid. I felt like I got robbed by someone I respected. I confronted the person, demanding a full refund. They tried to smooth talk their way out of it, offering only half of my money back for their "efforts." But I'm not one to be played. I remembered that I had paid with my credit card, so I contacted my provider and filed a dispute for services not rendered.

The day before my full $3600 was refunded to my credit card, I received a check in the mail from the person for $1800. Checkmate! Not quite. I ended up with my entire $3600 refund, and their check for $1800. Now I'm on top $1800. But I'm not about that dirty business, so I didn't cash their check. In the end, it wasn't just about the money, it was about fair business.

Amidst all of this, my marriage and other businesses were demanding attention, so OJ and I decided the timing wasn't right for R & O Wireless. The business never launched, but the lessons learned were invaluable.

I'm a hustler and I'm always down to make some additional legitimate cash to support my dream. At one point, I even dipped into buying and reselling goods, channeling the profits back into the business. But real estate is my business. It's in my blood.

I was twenty-six when I bought my first property which is major coming from where I'm from. But every journey's got its bumps. Some would call them challenges. I call them lessons.

I remember when I was selling my second property, still only 26 years old. My realtor dropped the ball big time. So that lit a fire under me. 'I can do this job better myself,' I thought. Next thing you know, I'm chasing my real estate license.

I found the listing of the house I was selling through her, and I was disappointed. It was just a simple description: Three bedrooms, two bathrooms, and two mango trees. No pictures. The house had been on the market for well over six months. I was steaming and I had to fire her ass. Once I got my license, I ended up selling my house myself. Get this, it only took me three months to sell it.

After getting my license in 2008, I teamed up with Keller Williams for a couple of years. The real estate market was on the rebound from the housing market crash due to the subprime mortgage crisis. I had only done a handful of business and my motivation was limited. But eventually, the itch came back, pushing me to another company, The REO Office. It was a small brokerage that specialized in foreclosures and bank owned properties. At the time, the market was flooded with these properties, and I was selling them like hot cakes all while learning and increasing my real estate knowledge. All was good with the company, but I felt like I was missing the technology aspect of the business and I really wanted to explore that side of the business. I later joined Exit Realty, continuing to balance my full-time job and work my real estate business.

My full-time job at CHS was supporting all my bills and household expenses. My commission checks from real estate transactions were all going to my savings account. I was doing pretty damn good. Looking at my commission check statement and seeing all the fees I was paying to the broker, I realized I could do my own thing and keep more of my commission. And then, that little voice said, 'Why not level up?'

I began to put my head back in the books and took the brokerage course. Despite everything I had going on, working two jobs, coaching etc., I dove right in. When I set my mind on a goal, it's nothing that can stand in my way or stop me from achieving it. After eight weeks, I completed the course, passed the state exam, and obtained my broker's license. I thought about buying a franchise with Exit Realty but realized they would control my game and I would still be kicking out serious cash in franchise fees.

In 2016, it was time for me to branch out and open Petty Capital Realty. While I was at Exit Realty, I took full advantage of the education they provided because I knew my end game. Absorbing knowledge was critical for my development in the real estate game and me starting my own brokerage. Legacy is everything! I was able to start and grow my brokerage to have huge success over the years. I was able to accomplish all of this by the age of thirty-seven.

Now, my degree in sociology? That was the key, man. It taught me to read and understand people, which is a golden attribute in the world of business. If you don't understand people, you're playing a losing game.

Let me tell you about this one investment deal under Petty Investments. There was this dude experiencing hardship, about to lose his house to foreclosure. He hit me up, asking if I would be interested in buying his house. He went on to explain that the house was being foreclosed within the next week and I would need to buy it fast.

He wanted to know that if I bought it, would I allow him to rent the home and allow him to buy it back from me within a year. I gave it some thought and agreed to do the deal with some terms. The terms included deadlines that needed to be met such as rental payments and a deadline to buy the home back within a year. If he failed to meet the terms, I would sell the home to secure my investment.

I provided him with the paperwork that included the terms and conditions and we both signed. Simple smooth deal. Well, it didn't quite go as smoothly as planned. Long story short is I helped him out, but things got sticky when repayment time came around. He was always late on the monthly rental payment, and he failed to buy the house back within the year as we agreed, so I extended the agreement for another year.

This dude had my money tied up for an additional year for which I did not plan. I'm not talking about a few hundred dollars, I'm talking about thousands, over $100k. After twists and turns, I sold the house because I needed my money to support other projects and deals that I was working on.

In spite of his shady business practices, I made sure I sold the home to a buyer that would allow him to live in the home. I could have sold it for much more if I wanted to, but I didn't. I ended up selling the house to a buddy of mine that would allow him to stay in the home just as I previously agreed with him. Sounds all good, right?

But nope! After all I did for him, he bad-mouthed me in the neighborhood, saying I stole his home. People know me, they know my character and they know I'm straight-up and not like that. Yet it stung.

Even if you do good, some will find a way to tarnish your name. That's business—it's not just about making a dollar; it's about helping people. It's about creating win-win situations. But that was a lesson I won't forget.

Yet, I've been able to accomplish and learn a lot on this journey of life. With *Petty Investments*, I've been on a mission buying up properties, and it's been a sweet ride to financial success.

One of my key business ambitions was what I call the *"10 Doors"* goal. Essentially, it means owning ten doors that would produce passive rental income. After crunching the numbers and figuring out the potential income and profits from the ten doors, the aim was clear in my mind and once I set my mind on a goal, it's a done deal.

I distinctly remember when I reached that milestone. I made a Facebook post, simply stating, "I did it." That was to mark the achievement of acquiring my tenth door of my 10-door goal. When I said, "I did it," I meant I now had ten doors which includes houses, duplexes, and condos. Each door is under my ownership, all generating income for me. It was a goal I had been working towards over the years, and finally, I had achieved it.

That is a taste of the success I've achieved. Those ten doors have bumped my net worth to exceed four million dollars. Man, that's something to be proud of. You get what I'm saying? To think, little ole me from Boynton Beach, Florida, was able to pull that off, it's a feeling of accomplishment, a real deep sense of pride. It just goes to show how far I've come.

Now, the golden question: "How do you balance all of this with a full-time gig?" Here's the real talk. We all got the same 24 hours in a day, but it's about the grind and how we use those 24 hours. We make excuses for things that we don't want to do. And we make exceptions for things that we want to do. So, one of the things that I make a point of not doing is making excuses. I keep going, you know what I mean? I like to say, "I don't make excuses, I make it happen."

It's about priorities, leveraging and balancing your time. Some days, the 9 to 5 is more like a nine to whenever. It's not always a walk in the park, but hey, I'm living proof it's possible.

I'm all about prioritizing. It's about squeezing every drop out of the 24 hours we all have. And yeah, it takes work, focus, and some late nights, but if I've learned one thing: you can't let excuses hold you back.

See, what you do between 9 to 5, that keeps the lights on, food on the table. But as I mentioned previously, your 5 to 9 hustle is where you build your dreams.

For me, it was diving deep into real estate. Every penny I made in those off-hours, I saved and reinvested it. I wasn't trying to keep up with the Joneses, but I treated myself here and there. Still, most of the money went right back into the game.

So, if you're looking for the secret sauce, it's being consistent, putting your priorities in order, using your time wisely, and never, ever making excuses. Scared money don't make money! You must do your homework and take calculated risks. Most importantly, you must believe in yourself. That's the Petty way!

PART FOUR
Family Ties & Personal Trials

Chapter Nine
Family:
The Core of Everything

Alright, y'all, let me bring you into my world for a moment. You see, while my life has been a roller coaster of hustles, dreams, and a touch of luck, there's always been this one constant that anchored me down, that kept me grounded. That one constant is family. Let me tell you, family is the essence, the core of everything I am today. It's the beat to my rhythm, the lyrics to my song.

Now, I'm always going to keep it 100. As a family, we've had our ups and downs, disagreements, fall-outs, all of it. But you see, the beauty of family is in its resilience. Socioeconomic, educational, and environmental challenges, our family has faced it all.

The value of resilience helped us navigate through adversity, bounce back from setbacks, and find strength in difficult circumstances. It's in the way we bounce back, come together, and lift each other up. Family is the foundation, the unshakable bond that has always given me purpose, direction, and most importantly, love.

As we dive into this chapter, I want y'all to feel the heartbeats, the laughter, the tears, and the lessons that come with this incredible journey. So, pull up a chair and let me share with you the essence of my world: my family.

Y'all know there's something sacred about family, right? The bond. The connection. There's just no replacing it. Now, remember my mom gave birth to me when she was young. She had her own set of challenges, her own journey, but I wouldn't trade her for the world.

Now, remember the dude I mentioned earlier? The one I was, let's say, *really* not vibing with. Well, after him, my mama took a step back, kind of cooled down a bit. Eventually, she settled with another man and I'm not gonna lie, it took me a good minute, probably five years, to even start a conversation with him. I was on my protective guard, you know. If anyone wronged my mama, I didn't want them thinking we were buddies or something.

So, when my mom would ask me if I was going to speak to him, I'd just stroll in and not utter a word. Looking back, it might've been some leftover anger from the times I felt like I had to step up and be the man. I was out here grinding, providing, and yet he was supposed to be her rock. So, why was I still handling business? It ate at me.

Now, my family knew how to manage me. If the dude ever said something slick or out of line, they'd shield me, knowing my temper, when it comes to my mama. Except for my auntie, she couldn't hold tea. Every now and then, she'd let something slip, and well, that would get my blood boiling. But over time, and with a few life experiences in between, we got to a somewhat okay place.

Seeing your mama navigate through tough times does something to you. It makes you protective. It puts you on edge.

There were times when I felt like if anything had to go down, I didn't want any emotional ties making it hard for me. If we were cool, there'd be that guilt, that remorse. But if we weren't, man I'd sleep like a baby, not losing a wink. If I had to handle a situation or hurt someone when it came to my mother, I would.

So, that's why I kept my distance for so long. I didn't want to mix feelings with what might need to be done. Crazy journey, right? Family and the intricate ties that bind us. It's something else.

Family is everything to me. It's our backbone, our core. The ones you can count on, no matter what storm life brings. My family, we're tight. Yeah, I got cousins, but let me tell you, we might as well be brothers and sisters with the bond we got. Growing up, it was always just us, holding each other down. Unity and togetherness within our family created a supportive and cohesive environment. Family members felt they could rely on each other for love, support, and guidance. We always understood that we were ONE and in this together!!

Life for me and my family was no cake walk growing up. All of us, my sister, brother, and cousins, we were all involved in the juvenile justice system at some point. You see, one thing about my family was we were going to do what we had to do to overcome a situation. The girls in our family were serious with their hands and if I had any problems with any other females, I knew I could call my sister or female cousins and they were ready for whatever.

There was a time when me and one of my friends had an argument about who's sister would win a fight. We got our sisters together and with no questions asked, they went at it. It was a good fight, but of course, my sister won. We still joke about it to this day.

And when it comes to my mama! Whew! If anyone, and I mean *anyone*, says a single bad word about me, they're about to catch her wrath. It doesn't matter if it's a friend or even a family member. Speak out of line about her boy and you'll

witness a mama bear ready to defend her cub. She'll look you dead in the eyes and make it clear: "That's my baby. I don't play about him!

It's all love, though. We're a close-knit bunch. From my siblings to my most distant cousin, there's this undeniable bond. They've got my back, and you best believe, I've got theirs. We look out for each other, always making sure we're good. That's what family does.

One thing about my family is the fact that although we faced numerous obstacles, we continue to persevere. The value of perseverance helped us persist through serious challenges, maintain our motivation, and work towards a better future.

One of those challenges lies in the disappearance of my Auntie Hattie, my mom's sister. It's like an open wound that never truly healed. This goes back to 1988, and though I only knew her for a short while, her absence has been deeply felt ever since.

Imagine this. One day, a 19-year-old pregnant girl just up and vanishes. No heads up, no warnings, no notes, nothing. One moment she's at the house, and the next moment, she's gone. She didn't even take her purse with her. It's like she just vanished into thin air. Nineteen. A baby herself, carrying another life inside her.

The details are chilling. Hattie's stepmother, Grandma Ruth was the last person known to have spoken to her. That very day, they had a chat over the phone. But when her stepmother got home, Aunt Hattie was nowhere to be found. And from that day in February 1988, not a single whisper of where she might've gone.

Hattie isn't just a statistic, another face on a missing person's poster, she is our blood. A young woman, standing at 5 feet 5 inches, weighing around 165 pounds, with soulful brown eyes and black, dark brown hair.

We've heard rumors over the years—whispers that she might be in California or maybe she returned home, but nothing concrete. No leads. A complete mystery. The haunting thought that keeps lingering is the fact that the last known person to have laid eyes on her was our own Granddaddy Ben. It led some folks in the family to wonder if he knew something. Maybe something happened right there, in his backyard. Thoughts like that can eat you up from the inside.

So, yeah, that's a chapter in our family history that's still very much open, still very raw. An ever-present reminder of how quickly our loved ones can just slip away.

With Aunt Hattie's sudden disappearance, the one lesson imprinted on our hearts was this: We are truly all we got.

Given the breaks and opportunities that I've been fortunate enough to have, I've made it my mission to ensure the same for every single member of our family. I'm all about rising and lifting others with me, so when I eat good, my family eats good. As I travel to the top, my family will be elevated too. When I win, we all win!

Now, I remember growing up and we didn't have fancy stuff. Hell, we didn't even have a car. But what we lacked in material possessions, we more than made up for it in love and unity. So, after my college days, I knew things had to change. The most basic of things, like a car can be a game changer in getting ahead in life. Without a ride, your job opportunities shrink. So, when it was time, my sis got her driving lessons from yours truly.

Man, that first time she got behind the wheel she nearly took out a trailer. We laugh about it now, but she learned: gas, brake, repeat. Not only did I teach her, but I bought her first set of wheels. First, the license, then her own car.

It didn't stop at my sister. Auntie was next in line. Auntie would always limit herself to job opportunities that were near public transportation. There wasn't a rideshare or Uber in those days. However, she wanted a change and better opportunities, and I knew the value a driver's license would bring her.

I remember teaching her the basics in a supermarket parking lot. I later set her up with a driving school, and after some hard work, she passed her test, and got a car. This led to endless opportunities for her. She was able to obtain a better job making more money. She soon started her own house cleaning business. Talk about transformation!

Now, Mama – that's another story. I took her to the same supermarket parking lot I took Auntie and taught her the basics of driving. I also signed her up for driving school. As hard as I tried, she just couldn't nail that written test. Still, stubborn as she is, I bought her a car. She had a few mishaps, a mailbox or two might've been casualties, but in the end, the car found its way to my sister Tasha.

Listen, my mama can be fiery, quick to tell you off if things don't go her way. Anyway, I bought her another car with the promise of her obtaining her license. Eventually, she lost the motivation to drive, and the car found its way to my Auntie.

Mama decided that she would use me and the family for her transportation. This made me think about how rich I could have been if I had only started this Uber business back then. I was doing the work for years and didn't make any big money. Damn, only if I knew then what I know now.

Uber would have been all me!

The ripple effect of it all is that my relatives, one by one, got their licenses, and their cars. Everyone was on the move, elevating, and pushing forward. As for me? Well, I have always been the family's unofficial banker and consultant. As long as I can remember I was the one they would entrust to hold their money. They knew early on that I was responsible with money and they never had to worry. They also knew I made pretty good decisions, so my advice was always valued.

I was the go-to guy for the family. Need to borrow money? Call Ricky. Need a legal document looked over? Call Ricky. Need a ride? Call Ricky. Need some advice? Call Ricky.

My family knows that whatever they may need, they can always call me, and I can most likely help or point them in the right direction.

Now, it doesn't stop at cars. Home ownership became another goal. After seeing my first house, my family became inspired. I took the time to educate them on the benefits as well as the process of buying a home and soon enough – bam!

One family member gets a house, then another, and another. We went from renting two-bedroom apartments to owning over seven million dollars collectively in real estate. Not bad at all, I guess that's the Petty way!

We haven't stopped there, because one thing about us Pettys, we know the power of knowledge. I'm talking about that big leap in the educational game. Now, I remember a time when Aunt Hattie was the only one I can recall rocking a high school diploma. Fast forward, and the game's all changed. We've been catching that wave of progress and riding it hard.

The family began to learn the importance of education and started to obtain their GEDs and high school diplomas. This led to better job opportunities. I like to think I had a hand in planting that seed and showing them the power of education.

Speaking of seeds, let's talk legacy. I kicked off a new family tradition by being the first to strut across the college stage. Now, I got fam shouting out "Let's go Wildcats!" Got young ones shoutin out, "I'm going to Bethune Cookman!" The pride is infectious, and we ain't slowing down. My children, Ricky Jr. and Rickia are both proud graduates of Bethune Cookman University and my younger daughter Rickiya will follow in their footsteps.

From me to my family, to the next generation, we're elevating, and it's a beautiful sight. We came from humble beginnings and as a family, we began to recognize the power of knowledge. We realized the importance of educating ourselves while seeking opportunities to learn, grow, and improve our socioeconomic status.

We embrace our cultural roots and take pride in our family. Our southern hospitality, good cooking, style, and good hearts run deep and help us maintain a strong sense of identity and rich cultural heritage. It's what makes us, us.

On occasional, I'd travel to South Carolina to vibe with our family there. But I noticed my family here in South Florida wasn't connecting as much. So, I hollered at my cousins one day. "Man, we gotta bring everybody together," I said. "We need a proper family reunion."

So, in 2008, I took the lead. I got everyone on board, and boom, our very first family reunion was in Spartanburg, South Carolina. Many of my family members had not been there to visit in quite some time. For many, it was their first time visiting.

The energy was pure magic! From that point on, it's been a tradition. One year, we're chilling in South Carolina, the next year, we're down here in Boynton Beach, Florida. And every time, it's nothing but love, laughter, and some good old family bonding.

There was a minute when my family didn't venture out too much. Like many people, they just stayed with what's familiar.

So, I thought, why not paint a bigger picture for them? Show them the vast world out there, waiting to be explored.

So later, we started hosting the family reunion in different places like Tennessee, New Orleans, Atlanta, and Key West. Then came the big leap, family cruises to the Bahamas and Mexico.

You know, because of where we came from, not everyone had passports, so I had to do some digging to find cruises where you didn't need all those fancy papers. Had to get smart about it, you feel me? But those cruises, man, it lit a spark. Got the fam buzzing! The Petty family is doing big things now like getting those passport stamps, crossing borders, exploring new horizons. Just the other day, I got a call from a family member. "Hey, just got my passport!" I couldn't help but smile because I remember when things were a lot different.

While we're talking growth, let's talk business. I saw the hustle in my family and thought, why not channel that energy? Why not level up? So, I started schooling them on the business game. "Y'all need to get an LLC, or maybe an S

Corporation," I advised. I began breaking down the benefits, laying them out step by step.

An LLC is a Limited Liability Company. The biggest win is right in the name – limited liability. This means if your business hits a rough patch, your personal assets are usually safe. Your car, your house, your personal bank account are not on the line if things go south. Plus, LLCs are flexible when it comes to taxes. You can choose how you want to be taxed, which can save you some serious cash.

Now, S-Corps, or S Corporations are a bit like LLCs but with some extra perks, especially when we talk about taxes. With an S-Corp, you can save on self-employment tax. How? Well, you can split your income between salary and dividends, and only the salary part gets hit with self-employment taxes. That's a smart way to keep more of your hard-earned money.

Another cool thing about S-Corporations is that they give you a bit of credibility. Having 'Inc.' after your business name can open doors, make you look more professional, and that can be a game-changer in attracting clients or investors.

Well, guess what? My family listened. Many of them now have their business entities all set up, and they're understanding the ins and outs of business.

I've been on this mission to not just elevate myself but bring my whole crew up with me. Give them tools, knowledge, a vision. Teaching them about the home ownership game, how to boss up in business, and basically how to maneuver through this wild ride called life. It's all about setting up for a better tomorrow, making moves, and crafting that dream life. And that's what we're doing, one step at a time.

I gotta lay it down about something real deep in the core of our family, that's our faith. Man, back in the day, we weren't always walking on that righteous path, you know what I mean? We weren't always *saved* and accepting Jesus Christ as our Lord and Savior; believing he died on the cross and rose from the grave. But when that moment hit, when we caught that revelation? Game changer.

Once we got saved, faith became our anchor and compass. Every stumble or hardship, we turned to our faith, and it held us up. It wasn't just about Sunday service or saying grace before meals, it became our everyday armor. Faith started moving in us, making us strong, giving us that bounce-back spirit. We learned to stand tall in the stormiest of days.

With faith, there's always that glimmer of hope, right? It gives us direction, fuels our purpose. It's a light guiding us through the dark, reminding us that no matter the odds, we know God is with us and has a plan for us. Every challenge, every tear, every joy, we know we're not walking alone. Our faith's got us, and we lean on it, drawing strength and resilience to face whatever life throws our way.

So yeah, faith is not just a word for us. It's our foundation, our rock, our daily dose of hope, purpose, and trust. It makes all the difference.

I want y'all to grasp what I've been laying down. The Petty family has a mixture of values, a blend that's been our playbook for life's wild game. I'm talking about that bounce back spirit. Resilience. Flipping a situation and making a dollar out of fifteen cents. It's resourcefulness. We got that grind and the drive to keep pushing. And man, we've got that unity, that togetherness. That's our secret sauce!

We ain't sleeping on knowledge either. Education and self-improvement are big players in our game. And of course, we got that unshakable belief and faith that's keeping us grounded. Can't forget that deep-rooted cultural pride and identity, reminding us of where we come from.

So, when y'all think of the Petty family, remember the essence, the heartbeats of our journey. And maybe, just maybe, y'all can vibe with some of these values as well.

Chapter Ten
Love Lessons

"If you're not at peace, if you're not happy, you can't operate at your best."

As we step into this next chapter, things get a touch deeper and a touch more personal. See, life ain't just about the hustle and the grind. At the core of it all, it's about love, connections, and sometimes, the painful lessons they bring. Love and loss have been the silent teachers in my life, guiding me, sometimes through joy, sometimes through pain.

Now, your boy's been through the whole spectrum. I've experienced the head-over-heels kind of love, the heart wrenching pain of goodbyes, and the journey back to self. My marriage was a dream, a vow to build the family I never had. But life, man, it is unpredictable.

Divorce isn't something you plan for, but it came knocking on my door, and I had to face it head-on and the healing. It was a journey back to me, but the road was full of bumps, curves, and detours.

In this chapter, I'm laying it all out, the highs, the lows, and the spaces in between. It's a deep dive into lessons of love, the bitter taste of loss, and the rebirth that follows. This is more than just a chapter in my book; it's a reflection of a heart that's loved, lost, learned, and lived.

As we move through these pages, I hope y'all find a little bit of your own journey reflected, understanding that through love and loss, we truly find ourselves.

Let's roll back the tape to '94, a year when ya boy felt that deep, magnetic pull for the first time. I was that dude on the field, suiting up for the Boynton Beach Bulldogs. She was that radiant cheerleader, glowing brighter than the rest. It's not like your boy didn't have admirers, being one of the top players came with its perks. But it was her, a dark, stunning beauty with a smile that would light up the darkest of nights.

We played this little game, flirtin' after practice, making silly bets. If we won our first game, she and I would kick it off official-like. If we lost? Nah, all bets were off. But destiny had its play, and after I scored two touchdowns, victory was in the bag.

From shared January birthdays to living a block apart from each other, our stars seemed aligned. Those long phone calls until dawn, the courtyard lunches, and the walks home. It felt like love was in the air.

Fast forward, she gave me two blessings, Ricky Jr., and Rickia. For them, my dreams soared high. I wanted that family picture, the kind I never had—a home with two parents holding it down. But as the years passed, life and love schooled me. The distinction between loving and being in love became crystal clear. Being loved was about feeling cherished, but being in love? That was a whole other universe of emotions, attachments, a kind of magic you can't quite describe.

My world was expanding, meeting new faces, diving into different cultures, climbing up the professional ladder. Yet, as I scaled new heights, I felt a widening gap. The woman who once walked beside me wasn't on the same journey anymore. The support, the understanding, it started to fade.

Although we were already midstream in our journey, 2009 was a defining year. We exchanged rings, said our vows, but man, life's no fairy tale. I played my part. I provided, I cared, and I even professed my love, but I also faltered. I allowed infidelity to creep into my relationship and that was something we could not get past. I offer no excuse and no justification. I'm not proud about it, but it's a chapter of my story, a lesson learned, and growth earned.

Now, let me tell y'all about the weight of ambition and how it tangled up with love in my life. As I rose in the business world, hitting milestones, carving out my legacy, I started feeling like I was on this climb solo. The woman I vowed to ride with seemed miles away. Every idea I threw, every plan I laid out, she'd counter it. Friction turned into full-blown fires, and her once devoted support felt like it was fading fast. We were driftin' like two ships in the night, and that divide got wider with every sunrise.

Now, to keep it 100, there were layers to our issues, it wasn't just business. Stuff we buried, old hurts, new pains, they played their part, making her put up walls, walls that became hurdles on my path to success. She failed to understand me as a man, the direction I was headed and the support I needed from her to get there. She would always complain about how busy I was or take issue with what I was doing. We just weren't on the same page. But here's where she got it twisted. Even with my calendar packed, the non-stop hustle, I never let home feel my absence.

When it came to our children, I was right there, coaching, school meetings, church on Sundays. Me and wifey, we had those golden moments – weekly dates, vacations, spontaneous trips. Home wasn't just a place I funded; it was my sanctuary. But that support, that mutual understanding, I felt like it was hanging by a thread.

Here I was, at a crossroads. I was pondering my life's path, wondering if this was the forever I'd envisioned. I love my family, and the life we built. It's a testament to the grind. But do I walk away?

Thoughts of the kids, the folks rooting for us, it all weighed heavy on me. The questions kept coming. Turning to God, we had deep conversations because I was searching for answers. I needed guidance, a beacon. It was time for some tough decisions, and faith was gonna be my compass.

The road to our divorce was heavy on my heart. There was a stretch where I was all in, trying to piece things together, fix the puzzle that was our marriage. You gotta understand, I'm all about family. I dreamt of a household that stayed tight, growing, and thriving together.

Growing up without both parents around, I knew deep down the value of having both mom and dad under one roof, giving children that solid foundation. But what hit me was the shadow side of staying in a bond gone sour. Our children, they were seeing it all—the heated exchanges, the cold silences. Witnessing moments that clashed hard with my vision of love and unity.

Neither one of us are saints in this story. Our decisions added to the storm. Talking felt like navigating a minefield. Trust was a memory, and unwavering support was nowhere in sight. I reached the breaking point. As I stared at the mirror of our relationship, I realized it was time to choose. Either I keep pushing through the fog or find clarity. Making the choice to part ways, to step into a new chapter was about healing, for both of us and for our family's future.

After the rollercoaster of my marriage, I can tell you, there are some non-negotiables if you're aiming for that lasting, deep kind of love. Let me break it down for y'all.

Shared faith and beliefs. That's huge. Sharing a spiritual connection, having deep-rooted beliefs that align, it's vital. It's like that old saying, "A family that prays together, stays together." That's real talk. When you're seeing eye to eye on things that matter, like faith and values, it creates a solid foundation. It's not just about going to church or saying prayers, it's about living those beliefs in your life, supporting each other in your spiritual journey. That shared faith weaves a bond that can help weather any storm. It's a core part of the glue that holds everything together.

Then there is *communication.* It's more than just talking; it's really about being heard and listening to each other. It's about keeping it real, being genuine, and tackling issues head-on, no masks, no pretense.

Then comes *trust.* I'm talking bedrock-level foundation here. This means being the person your spouse can rely on, keeping your word, and making sure they never have to doubt your intentions.

Respect is massive. Recognizing and valuing each other's opinions, space, and choices, that's the game. Although you both are united as one, each person is an individual, and in marriage, it's like a dance where both lead, and both follow.

Now, *commitment* ain't just about rings and vows. It's an everyday choice. It's sticking together, pushing through the storms, and never letting go, even when the journey gets rough.

Relationships aren't all sunshine, so *emotional support* is key. Being that safe haven for your partner, standing with them through highs and lows, and giving them that shoulder is priceless.

You ask yourself, what's steering the relationship? It should be shared values and goals that keep you on the same page, sharing dreams and visions, creating the team spirit that keeps the relationship alive.

Quality time and intimacy, I can't stress this enough. It's about those stolen moments, shared laughter, and the deep connection, both in mind and body.

Every relationship will test you, so having *flexibility and compromise* is clutch. It's about coming together, making those little adjustments, and ensuring the harmony keeps playing.

Then, it's all about *continuous growth and learning*. Keeping the fire that keeps you evolving, bettering yourselves, and growing together, that's what keeps the bond fresh and exciting.

Lastly, but never least, is *forgiveness*. Everyone slips, everyone falters. Holding onto past mistakes is like poison. Letting go and moving forward is where healing and growth thrive.

Looking back, these aren't just values, these are lifelines, the heartbeats of what I believe makes a healthy relationship stand the test of time. Hold onto them, and you'll find the love you're searching for.

As for me, when I think about my journey through love, it feels like I've walked a thousand miles uphill, in the snow, with no shoes on. But hey, those miles gave me the wisdom I've got now.

You see, a healthy relationship is like life itself. You have to be willing to put in the work. You're the artist, and that canvas can either be a masterpiece or a doodle. It all boils down to the strokes you choose.

Oh, I had my days under the sun, moments when everything felt like it was pulled out from a fairy tale. But, just like every story, mine had its twists and turns also. I ain't gonna front, I made some choices, choices that shook the very foundation of my marriage. But that's the thing about life, right? It's all about the lessons.

Every sunrise, every sunset, every tear, every laugh, they've all taught me something. Now, if you're looking for some sage advice, having walked this path, here's what I've got for you. Embrace the eleven values I shared earlier. Let them be your North Star. But if you ever find yourself in a space where those core values are getting trampled upon, pause, and ask yourself these questions. *"What's the cost to my peace? What's the cost to my happiness?"* There's a heavy price tag on compromising those.

If you find your joy dimming, your peace disturbed, then you've got to reassess. I would tell anyone, and I mean anyone: never let someone steal your sunshine.

If you're not at peace, and if you're not happy, you can't operate at your best, and if you can't operate at your best, you can't give your best. Understand this, you can't pour from an empty cup. If you are broken and operating out of anger, frustration, and unhappiness, you're not going to live your best life. FACTS.

Healing after a divorce is like mending a broken bone. It hurts, the healing process is slow, and it's a journey only *you* truly understand. I won't sugarcoat it. I went through a whirlwind of emotions. You have those moments where you're lying awake at night, second-guessing your decisions, wondering if the world's looking at you sideways.

But healing isn't linear. It's a process. And just like any wound, you need to give it time. There were days I felt like a shadow, lost in the hustle and bustle of life, wondering if I'd ever feel full again. I mean, how do you pour from an empty cup?

Then it hit me. I had to flip the script. Instead of worrying about filling other people's cups, it was time to focus on my own. You see, diving into self-care is more than bubble baths and spa days, it's a full-on commitment to your physical, mental, and spiritual wellbeing. I had to dust off those old dreams, set up new goals, and really start living for me. From hitting the gym, focusing on my businesses, to finding that inner peace. I was on a mission.

You can't forget what brings you joy. There is something healing about giving back, spending quality time with family, and just exploring the world. It's like every moment breathes life back into you. But a crucial part of my bounce back was my circle. A tight-knit group of confidants who had my back, gave me those reality checks, and just let me vent when needed.

In a nutshell, healing is a journey, not a destination. And with patience, a lot of self-love, and the right folks by your side, you'll find your way back to the sunshine. Trust me on that.

When we talk about the essence of commitment, especially in the realm of romantic relationships, there are some folks who've deeply sculpted my outlook on it and man, have they made a mark!

On the spiritual side: Let's talk about the McCurdys. I've had the blessing of knowing them since my knee-high church days. The vibe they emanate is undeniable. They've always been deep in their faith, hands-on in church work. Whether it's about being stellar parents, top-notch professionals, or just good souls, they had it down. I've never seen a storm cloud hang over them, it's rays of positivity and togetherness. Their unity is seamless! Watching their journey, their commitment to God and to each other, it laid down the blueprint for what I saw as unwavering commitment.

And speaking of people who resonate the same kind of spiritual depth and authenticity, Mr. & Mrs. Bush come to mind. Their style and grace and their devotion to life is something I deeply admire. They are the epitome of being God-fearing and stylish. They exemplify the tenacity needed in marriages. They're always ready to offer a prayer or a piece of advice, illuminating the path for others. Their loyalty to each other is profound, showcasing the true essence of love – vibrant, exciting, and full of fun.

Now, shifting to the business world: Enter the Ross family. The energy they bring, it's infectious. Mrs. Ross is fierce, a powerhouse who takes no prisoners when business is on the table. Mr. Ross is the backbone. He makes sure the ship sails smoothly. Both are pillars in education and still juggling a slew of businesses.

I've seen their ascent, watched as they balanced work, community service, and a beautiful family. They don't make excuses, they're doers, movers, and shakers. Their mojo? It's a mix of unwinding, pouring love into their bond, handling their ventures, and nurturing their family. They're the embodiment of commitment in love and work, and man, do I look up to them!

These couples always have rays of positivity and togetherness. Their unity is seamless! Watching their journeys, their commitment to each other and God, it laid down the blueprint for what I saw as unwavering commitment.

The Bush, the McCurdy, and the Ross families, they're not just about success; they're about building something meaningful, something lasting – in business, in community, and especially in love.

When I think about love's horizon for me, I see nothing but sunshine and clear skies. I've walked the path, stubbed my toes a couple of times, but I've learned. Most importantly, I've taken a deep dive into the man in the mirror. I've mapped out the things I desire, as well as the things I won't even entertain anymore.

Love's a two-way street, and by now, I've got a Ph.D. in it. I've decoded its language, and I know what it takes and what it gives. I've come to cherish the pillars that make relationships healthy—that's right, my eleven values. They're not just words, they're the compass guiding my journey.

If marriage is what you desire, please know that it is not a seasonal gig. Marriage is for life. It's the kind of marathon you run side by side with your partner, matching each other's stride. It's that masterpiece you both paint, one brushstroke at a time.

I've set a lavish table on my love journey. My future wife will not only have a seat but will add to its grandeur. I can already see her glow. She's going to be over the moon!

Now, I believe in that old scripture, Proverbs 18:22, "*He who finds a wife finds what is good and receives favor from the Lord.*" But remember, it's not just about finding the one, it's about being ready to dance to the rhythm of love together. That synergy, that bond – it's gold. Keep the channels of communication flowing, anchor your trust, and chase those dreams together. Dive deep into love, stay submerged, and remember you're a duo, unbeatable, unbreakable.

I could go on, but I don't want to preach. If ever in doubt, circle back to my core values. They're my roadmap. Perhaps they'll light a path for others. Cheers to the journey ahead!

PART FIVE

Living the Dream

"*Live Life To The Fullest Because It Only happens*

Once"

Maddi Jenkins

Chapter Eleven
Triumphs in the Business World

"Every triumph starts with a decision to try."

When you talk about the highs and lows, the rollercoaster of the business world, I've been on that ride! Welcome to "Triumphs in the Business World," the chapter where I pull back the curtain on my journey, from the initial spark of an idea to building a legacy.

Growing multiple businesses wasn't a walk in the park. There were nights when the weight of responsibility felt like a 100-pound vest, but then there were days where the sun shined so brightly on my ventures that I had to pinch myself. From the small business setup to expanding operations that touched different corners of the globe, I've seen it, done it, and got the t-shirt.

But hold on, it's not just about the glamorous success stories. I've had my fair share of missteps and lessons that came at a price. Every hurdle taught me something new, sharpened my strategy, and fine-tuned my vision. In these pages, I'll share the wisdom collected from the school of hard knocks, giving you a front-row seat to the plays that worked and those that... well, let's just say they offered "growth opportunities."

Never, and I mean never, let your dreams slip through your fingers. I had this big vision of owning multiple properties. My first shot at this was a duplex in Boynton Beach, a really nice place with two bedrooms on each side. So, I hit up a loan officer to see if I could swing a mortgage for it. The asking price was $145k. So, we do the dance. I provide all the info, and bam, I get the approval letter. We negotiated, and I locked it in at $130k. Man, I was on cloud nine, under contract and all.

Then I start rolling through the process – inspection,

appraisal, sending over documents, then out of nowhere, things start going south. The loan officer hits me up, says my debt-to-income ratio's too high. I cleared my credit card debts, but it wasn't enough. So, I'm thinking, I gotta make this work. I had just copped a brand-new Chevy Camaro, my pride and joy, only four months old. 'If I sell the car, maybe, just maybe, it'll tip the scales.' So, I rushed to the dealership, desperate style. They lowball me, of course, but I'm focused on that duplex. I let go of my Chevy, a tough call, but I'm all in.

I update the loan officer, she reruns the numbers, and things look good. But check this, one day before closing, the owners bail, talking about some bank agreement they can't sidestep. Man, I was hot, actually I was furious, angry, you name it. I'd poured cash into this, lost money on fees, cleared debts, even said goodbye to my Camaro. I made some serious sacrifices and after all I had done, it was still not enough.

But like I always say and believe, never throw in the towel on your dreams. Fast forward a few years later, and guess what? I ended up snagging that very duplex, and yeah, I paid a lot more than the initial deal, but I understood the game. And not just that one, I bagged the duplex next to it as well. Two duplexes side by side and I own them both. That's how you do it! That's the power of keeping your eyes on the prize, no matter what life throws at you. Look at God working!

In the business world, there are always curveballs. Being prepared for these unforeseen challenges is crucial. Mistakes will happen, poor choices will be made, but most importantly, lessons will be learned.

I recall my early days in the house flipping game, a lucrative venture for those who understand the rules and have a solid plan. This game is not for the weak and thank God I'm built for it because one of my deals turned into a nightmare.

I had an opportunity to purchase a property at a really good price. After I completed my assessment of the property, I remember thinking, 'this is a damn good deal.' All was looking well. The property was a four-bedroom, two-bathroom home with a pool. It had ample yard space in a nice neighborhood. It needed some rehab work and upgrades: a new roof, updated bathrooms and kitchen, pool maintenance, landscaping, interior and exterior paint, and some stucco work. My initial estimate for the renovations was around $60k, which left plenty of room to make a profit.

In this game and how my mind is wired, I make my money when I buy the property, so buying at the right price is key. So, I purchased the property and began the renovation process. I was referred to a guy who supposedly was a general contractor. I didn't do any research on this guy, big mistake. He quoted me a great price of $30k for the job and promised a three-week turnaround time. It was half the price of the estimated cost I'd tallied up, so I thought it was a sweet deal. Another red flag.

Excited by the prospect, I signed the contract and paid the deposit. Two weeks later, I swung by the property to find that he hadn't even started. He fed me a story about being tied up on another job and he gave me his roofer's contact, Michael Jackson, a name I'll never forget.

I met with the roofer, paid a $5000 deposit, but then, silence. Weeks passed without any progress. Frustrated, I confronted the contractor about the lack of actions by him and the roofer. Two months in, with minimal work done on the project that was supposed to take three weeks, I was bleeding time and money.

I continued to reach out to the roofer, but no answers. The roofer had me so hot and upset, to the point of me thinking crazy, I was ready to get into some gangster shit. It really wasn't about the money; it was about the principles. I felt this dude had really tried me like a sucka, and it was a struggle because my pride didn't want to let it go.

I thought about having my girl call him from another number for a roof estimate and when he showed up, give him the left right left right combo. After all that was going on and some serious consideration, I realized it wasn't worth risking my freedom over a few dollars and the principle of the situation.

I decided to put my pride aside, cut my losses and keep it moving. I fired the so-called general contractor, brought in a reliable team, and pushed ahead.

Although the project resulted in a substantial financial hit, it was a profound learning experience. I learned the importance of having a trustworthy, skilled team. Michael Jackson and the so-called general contractor could not be trusted nor were they solid or committed to the work. Since then, I've assembled a reliable crew, from general contractors to roofers, electricians, plumbers, painters etc.

I learned a very valuable life lesson from this deal. It's simple: "You have to make more money than you do mistakes." But despite the setbacks, I managed to cover my losses and even turn a profit. It was a tough but valuable lesson on the importance of careful planning and team selection in business.

So, for all you promising entrepreneurs out there with fire in your belly and dreams as vast as the sky, this one's for you.

Dive into my story, extract the gems, and remember, every triumph starts with a decision to try.

Thinking back to those early days and the dreams that danced in my young mind. Like many kids, the glitz and glamour of the NFL shined in my eyes. 'That's success,' I thought. But as time passed, the tune of my heart changed. The hustle of the streets, the allure of quick money from selling drugs, I soon realized that wasn't my song. I wanted more, a life where money wasn't the daily worry, where I could step into my truth.

I had once looked up at the sky, dreaming of standing tall and proud among the ranks of the Marines. I was always fascinated with the Marines. I loved their work ethic and their character building. I believe it is such an honor to serve in the U.S. Military and put your life on the line for our country. I salute every soul that is serving or has served in our armed forces.

I would have loved to be among those men and women, but life threw me curveballs. My run-ins with the law meant those wings got clipped before they could even spread. Hard, manual labor? Nah, that wasn't me. I wasn't built to cut grass under the sweltering sun or to toil away in odd jobs. My spirit yearned for more.

Early on, it was crystal clear what I didn't want. But pinpointing what I wanted, well, that took a minute. From the creativity of architecture to capturing life's moments as a photographer, and even stepping into a courtroom as a lawyer, different dreams flickered in and out.

But do you know what became clear as day? My genuine passion to inspire, uplift, and add value to others, that's my mission. Whatever I did, it had to touch souls, uplift my community, and pave a better path than the one I walked on. It was more than just elevating my life; it was about uplifting those around me. I looked at the struggles in my community, the challenges my family faced, and I wanted to be that beacon of hope, the living proof that dreams are valid.

To be successful in life, you've gotta grasp the essence of discipline and the necessity of sacrifices. I've always had a dream of owning a Black Corvette. I'd daydream about cruising down the intercoastal, looking east at the Atlantic Ocean in that sleek ride with the top down, soaking in the South Florida breeze and vibing to my tunes. Eventually, I reached a point in my life where I was patting myself on the back. 'Mr. Wonderful, you've earned this,' I thought to myself. 'Time to treat yourself to that dream car.'

I had just flipped a property, made a sweet profit, and was all set to hit the dealership. But life threw me a curveball. Got a call about a condo for sale, a place with real potential, needing some work but nothing beyond my skillset.

As much as that Corvette was calling my name, I had to step on the brakes. Discipline. Sacrifice. I chose to pass on the car and move on the condo deal instead. Negotiated a fair price, making it a win-win situation for the seller and myself. That's my style.

Got the condo and hit the ground running with a total rehab. New tile floors, bathroom, kitchen, appliances, the works. It was immaculate. I thought about flipping it, but then, considering my goal of building up my real estate portfolio (10 Doors), I decided to keep it as a rental.

Long story short, when I commit to something, I make it happen, no matter what. And the dream car, the black Corvette—I bought it the following year. And you know what's sweet, the income from the condo covered the cost of it! Just think about the financial hit I would've taken if I hadn't exercised discipline. If I hadn't made the sacrifice, I would have missed out on a prime asset and the opportunity to earn appreciation value and passive income.

I'm just grateful. I'm grateful to God for blessing me with wisdom, for guiding me through these choices. The decision I made allowed me to leverage my assets and finally snag my dream ride.

Success, to me wasn't just a fat bank account, luxury things, or fancy titles, it was about quality of life, inner peace, and being a well-rounded individual. That's my dream, and every step I take is in pursuit of that vision. So, here's to chasing passions, rewriting narratives, and sculpting success from the clay of ambition.

Understand that I put my heart into my work, but I can't deny the fact that if I dedicated even more focus, the potential for growth is astronomical. I'm juggling so many ventures, and it's clear I need to hone in on my priorities. The thing is, even without major advertising for Petty Capital Realty, even without aggressive recruiting, I've managed to bring on more agents than many who are out there hustling hard.

People see my passion and drive and consequently, they approach me, wanting to join forces. I sit with them, ensuring we're aligned in vision and purpose because if it's not the right fit, I guide them to other avenues that might suit them better.

Petty Capital Realty isn't just a business, it's a pillar of the community. From its inception to its rise, this venture has been about more than just bricks and mortar and selling homes. From the days when I was the sole force behind it, we've scaled mountains. Now, boasting multi-million dollar deals annually, our team has swelled from a one-man show to a powerhouse ensemble of over twenty agents. And let me be straight with you, we're not just competing, we're leading. Our brand, meticulously carved over the years, stands tall and is a testament to dedication, grit, and passion.

But here's the thing, success, in my book, isn't just about the transactions or the acclaim, it's about the impact. *Petty Capital Realty* is a vessel, one that allows me to pour back into our community and others. Beyond the deals, we're consistently laying foundations in our neighborhoods, donating to numerous organizations, fueling events, and sparking hope in the next generation. Whether I'm at the podium sharing insights or on the ground at sporting events, the aim remains – uplift, inspire, and make a difference.

And speaking of blessings, because of the success and the understanding of my roots, I've transformed the housing narratives for many in my tribe. Many of my kin, who once knew only rented spaces, now proudly hold keys to their own homes, building not just houses, but legacies. To see them flourish, to witness the pride that comes with home ownership, and to know they're building equity and generational wealth, that's real success. It's milestones like these that underscore the growth and essence of Petty Capital Realty.

Overall, business has been kind to me, and much of that comes from my extensive network. The relationships I've fostered, the knowledge I've gleaned from others, it's all invaluable. I make it my business to study others, learning from both their triumphs and missteps, ensuring I sidestep common pitfalls.

But here's a nugget of wisdom I've held close: having a vision and sticking to it is paramount. Most folks falter because they either lack a plan or stray from it. At the end of the day, it's about making a plan and working the plan. It might sound rudimentary, but success can often be boiled down to following steps A, B, and C. Where others complicate the simple, I find clarity, removing the complicated into practical pieces.

The importance of financial planning can't be overstated. Operating without a budget is like sailing without a compass. Investing in oneself is pivotal. If you aren't willing to pour into your skills, into your growth, you're setting yourself up for stagnation.

Sometimes, it's about realizing you don't have to shoulder everything. Why create another job for yourself? The objective is to streamline operations, create efficient systems, and, most importantly, work smarter, not harder.

Time is currency. Why invest eight hours doing something that could be outsourced at a fraction of your worth?

Recognizing this transformed my work ethic, making me more proficient. Solid communication, humility, and the ability to sometimes move silently have been integral in my journey.

When I was just starting out, a thought popped into my head. 'Ricky, how much are you worth? How much is your time per hour?' I had to do the math, then I asked myself, why grind for eight hours on something that could be handled by someone else, especially if it costs me less than what I could make during that time? That one lightbulb moment reshaped how I approached work. Couple that with keeping my lines of communication open, being consistent, remaining humble, and making moves in silence. That's been the recipe for my success.

But with success comes its own set of challenges, and pitfalls you can't always see coming. They hit you out of the blue, leaving you to sit back and really reflect on life and its unpredictable ways.

Covid hit the world like a ton of bricks, touching lives everywhere, mine was no exception. It was Christmas Eve 2020 when it started for me. I had a headache, but I brushed it off, kept pushing through the day, getting ready to play Santa for my little girl. We baked cookies for Santa, and after tucking her in, I set up her gifts around the Christmas tree – bikes, dolls, a Barbie Kitchen, the works.

When she woke up, her smile was everything. Pure joy!

We had a blast that day, riding bikes, playing house. Later, we dropped off gifts to family members and met up with her siblings. After a day full of family time, we headed back home. That night, as we were getting ready for bed, my lady, Lena tells me I'm burning up. I seemed to have a fever. I brushed it off again, thinking it was nothing. But then my daughter, she starts feeling sick too. "Daddy, my tummy hurt," she said. I felt bad and stayed up with her.

The next day, after dropping my daughter off home to spend time with her mother, I felt wiped out. Lena was convinced it was Covid. She started sanitizing everything, while I'm quarantined in our room. The next morning, I received a call from my frat brother, and he confirmed my fears, he tested positive for Covid.

I hustled to get tested, shelling out $200 to skip the long lines, and yep, the test came back positive. We both had attended a Christmas party a few days earlier and we assumed that is where we were exposed to the virus. I immediately let everyone that I'd been in close contact with know, but it was too late for my daughters. They both had tested positive also. That made me feel even worse.

For the next week, I was stuck at home. I'm usually always on the move, but Covid slammed the brakes on that. I had to miss being courtside at the Miami Heat game. I had an opportunity to sell the tickets, but instead, I gave them to a worthy couple who would cherish the experience.

Despite missing the game, the downtime wasn't all bad. I read, watched movies, lounged by the pool, just letting it all hang out. For once, I was worry-free, focused solely on me. It gave me time to reflect on life, business, and family. It's wild how life can be so fragile. It really hit me—don't take anything for granted.

On my journey in the world of business I have learned a lot. From all my experiences, I've distilled a few core lessons.

- Communicate effectively.

- Establish clear expectations.

- Be consistent; follow up and follow through.

- Always have a plan, a roadmap to your destination.

- Understand the significance of budgeting.

Ultimately, success is subjective. For me, it's about happiness, peace, and the absence of helplessness. It's about accomplishing goals, helping others, and having financial freedom. Every day brings new tasks, new challenges, but with a clear vision and unwavering dedication, those lofty dreams are within arm's reach.

Navigating success isn't a roll of the dice, it's grounded in age-old principles. Allow me to enlighten you with some tried and true insight. In the world of wealth-building, there are roads less traveled, and then there are highways. To give you a clearer picture, let's delve into the four methods of the Petty's Cash Playbook:

- *Earned Income:* Envision this as the foundational layer. It's that day-to-day grind, the 9 to 5 commitment. It's consistent, yes, but is it the only stairway to wealth? I suggest you think again.

- *Passive Income:* Now we're talking! Imagine sowing a seed once, then sitting back and enjoying its fruits season after season. My venture, Petty Investments, is a testament to this. It's yielding dividends even when I'm deep in dreamland. Dive deeper, and you'll find realms like dividend-yielding stocks, real estate investments and rental properties.

- *Portfolio Income:* This is the refined move, the chess game of finance. It's where stocks, bonds, life insurance, and annuities converge. When you decode this matrix, the windfall can be phenomenal. Need clarity? Picture earnings from real estate deals, mutual fund dividends, royalties from patents, stock market gains, or bond interests.

- *Compound Interest:* My ace in the hole! Einstein wasn't jesting when he labeled this the "eighth wonder." Reflect on his wisdom: "He who understands it, earns it ... he who doesn't ... pays it."

This isn't just about earning, it's about letting your earnings amplify themselves, relentlessly. To break it down, think of regular savings accounts, retirement portfolios, or stocks that keep appreciating.

This has been my compass to prosperity. Remember, the beauty of the journey isn't just in the destination, but in the lessons and strategies that guide us there. Absorb this, let it resonate, and when the moment feels right, march forth, illuminated by these guiding principles.

If there's one other thing I've learned from grinding in the hustle of entrepreneurship, it's that success isn't handed to you on a silver platter, you have to go get it.

Since you made it this far in the book, I would like to reward you with a few nuggets of wisdom from my journey that will give you a leg up.

- *You Got to Believe:* It's crucial to have unwavering confidence – in yourself, your team, and your business vision. Believing is the first step to achieving. When you're firmly rooted in this belief, you tackle challenges head-on and inspire those around you to do the same.

- *Start With the End in Mind:* Start by envisioning your ultimate goal. This clear-end vision will guide your decisions and actions, acting like a roadmap for your journey. Break it down into smaller, achievable steps, which keeps you focused and on track towards your desired destination.

- *Passion Over Profit:* It might sound cliché, but you must be passionate about what you do. If your heart ain't in it, the challenges will knock you flat. But if you wake up every day driven by passion, there's no obstacle too big.

- *Stay Hungry, Stay Humble:* Remember those early days when you were just starting, the hunger, the drive? Hold onto that. No matter how successful you are, never forget where you came from. Humility will keep you grounded.

- *Learn to Pivot:* Not every idea is going to be a slam dunk. Sometimes, you've got to pivot, adapt, and reimagine and that's okay. It's all part of the dance.

- *Build a Solid Team:* No one has ever achieved anything great by themselves. Your team is your backbone. Surround yourself with people who share your vision, but don't be afraid of those who challenge you. Different perspectives can ignite the most groundbreaking ideas.

- *Take Calculated Risks:* Entrepreneurship is about taking risks, but not flying blind. Do your research, weigh the pros and cons, but don't be paralyzed by over-analysis. Sometimes, you just gotta take that leap of faith.

- *Celebrate the Small Wins:* It's not just about the end game. Celebrate the milestones along the way. They'll fuel your spirit and keep that fire burning bright.

- *Never Stop Learning:* The world's changing fast. What worked yesterday might not work tomorrow. Stay on your toes, keep educating yourself, and be ready to evolve.

- *Listen More Than You Speak:* Sometimes, the best insights come from just listening to your customers, your team, even your competitors. Keep those ears open.

- *Mind Your Mental Health:* Burnout is real. Take care of your mental well-being. When things get heavy, don't be afraid to take a step back and rejuvenate. Your business needs you at your best.

- *Remember Your 'Why:* When things get tough and trust me, they will, remember why you started. Let your purpose be your north star, guiding you through the darkest nights.

There you have it. The road to entrepreneurship is a marathon, not a sprint. Lace up those shoes tight, stay the course, and above all, enjoy the ride. Because, trust me, it's one heck of a journey.

ENTREPRENEURIAL CHARACTERISTICS
Personal
Kitapping
Point

Chapter Twelve
Embracing Life Now

"Now, while faith is the compass, the terrain of life requires a steady mind."

We've journeyed through the come-up, the grind, and the hustles that carved out my path. But where has that path led me?

Right here, right now. Let's park it and take a minute to breathe, to reflect, to just be. Life's been a whirlwind, but when you're living it pedal-to-the-metal, sometimes you've got to ease off the gas, take in the scenery, and chart out the next stretch of road.

Now, if you're picturing me lounging in some plush penthouse sipping on something aged, well, you're not entirely wrong. But there's more to the story. It's not all glam and glitter. There are moments of introspection, reviewing lessons learned, and the sweet simplicities of life. It's late-night musings and sunrise aspirations. It's the blend of yesterday's dreams with tomorrow's ambitions.

In this chapter, we're diving in, headfirst. I'm unlatching the doors to my current world, shedding light on past reflections, offering a sneak peek into my present rhythms, and dishing out the dreams that drive my tomorrows.

So, as we bridge the gap from my roots to my reality, let's also muse over the horizons I'm setting my sights on, because believe me, this ride is just getting started. You with me?

Let this sink in. At the time of this writing, the life expectancy for all men hovers around 76 years, while for Black men, it's close to 71 years. The retirement age in the United States is 67. Crunch those numbers, and there's a glaring truth—I might not even get a taste of retirement, let alone savor it. Now that's a raw deal in my book. So, here's my play: I'm seizing life, full throttle, right now! I'm jet-setting, basking in life's finest offerings, and yet, staying anchored to my core mission—enriching lives and leaving an indelible impact. How about that for a game plan?

Let's explore how I have shaped a life, not just of success, but of substance and significance. 'Being Petty' isn't just a tagline for me, it's an intricate tapestry of values, beliefs, and habits I've woven over the years.

Central to the beauty of my life is faith. There's an indomitable strength that comes from recognizing and revering a force grander than oneself. And while this belief is personal, the journey isn't solitary. My spiritual anchorage finds its home at Greater St. Paul A.M.E. Church in Boynton Beach, Florida. Being an active part of this faith community has gifted me with an avenue to actualize my purpose, extending its impact beyond my immediate surroundings.

Now, while faith is the compass, the terrain of life requires a steady mind. I've always championed the significance of a positive mindset. Happiness isn't merely a feeling, it's a cultivated habit. Whether it's anchoring oneself in gratitude, cradling self-compassion, or championing a growth-centric  perspective, the mind is the garden, and positivity, its perennial bloom.

But, what's a journey without fellow travelers? Relationships have been the bedrock of my existence. From the embrace of family and friends to the warmth of a supportive community, these bonds have bestowed upon me a sense of belonging and unyielding emotional support.

The hustle, as exhilarating as it is, demands balance. This equilibrium isn't just about work, it extends to leisure, personal time, and the soul-refreshing moments in between. I revel in the symphonies of self-care, from the immersive tunes of my favorite hobbies to the quiet interludes I spend with my loved ones.

Speaking of care, mental well-being isn't just a footnote, it's a headline. From the therapeutic cadence of sports and exercises to the rejuvenating intermissions of vacations, each step I take is calibrated to ensure a mind at peace, resilient against life's unpredictable tempests.

Now, a sound mind deserves a temple. My physical health isn't just a responsibility, it's a ritual. Be it the rhythmic routines of exercise, the deliberate choices of nourishing meals, or the reassuring visits to the doctor, each action is a testament to a commitment to longevity and vitality.

The journey of life isn't static, it's dynamic. And so, personal development is my North Star. With an insatiable thirst for knowledge, I continuously chart courses into the realms of growth, be it through strategic learning or seeking out experiences that refine the essence of who I am.

Finally, the 'Petty Way' finds its crescendo in giving. The joy of success is magnified when shared. Whether it's lending a hand, sharing a smile, or championing a cause, every act of kindness amplifies the symphony of happiness and fulfillment in my life's narrative. *To whom much is given, much is required.* Over the years, I have been blessed beyond measure and it is my pleasure to serve and give back.

As I continue to balance life, one of my favorite pastimes is traveling. Traveling is more than just a hobby for me, it's a passion, a balm, a teacher. I've had the privilege of dipping my toes in many foreign shores. There's a special kind of magic in journeying beyond the familiar territories of home.

The sweet spot is the joy of sharing those experiences with the next generation. I've been blessed to take my children along on several of these voyages, letting them see, feel, and understand the world outside their usual sphere. You see, as a father, my aim is to open up worlds for them that I could only dream of as a child.

The sparkle in their eyes as they take in these new experiences is priceless. And it's not just about the travels, it's about becoming the man and father I've always aspired to be. Today, I stand before them and you, equipped mentally, physically, financially, and spiritually to lead by example.

Imagine this: a young boy from humble beginnings not even able to attend summer camp, dreaming of being able to live a life where I didn't have to struggle. That was me. And then, fast forward to that same boy, now a man, standing amid the towering skyscrapers of Dubai, getting lost in the serenity of the Greek isles, and being captivated by Italy's rich tapestry of art and history.

No words can truly capture the high I get, experiencing what used to be just dreams inked in my old schoolbooks. The blend of breathtaking landscapes, mouth-watering dishes, ageless art, and diverse cultures are experiences that are now part of my soul's tapestry.

My desire to travel hasn't been satisfied. Oh no, it's ever growing. My eyes are set on bigger dreams now. Picture a map of the world, with pins on each continent, marking major cities. That's the plan. To touch, feel, and embrace every piece of this vast, beautiful world. And I'm already off to a great start.

Let me keep it 100 with y'all. I'm out here truly living my best life, soaking in every bit of the goodness life's got lined up for me. Peace? Man, that's my anchor. Every day, it's all about leveling up, being that better version of me. Spiritually, mentally, physically, and yep, financially – it's all growth, all the time.

I've been blessed to jet-set across the globe, experiencing places most only dream about. I've felt the electrifying energy of watching a Miami Heat game courtside. I've experienced VIP sideline treatment at Miami Dolphins games. I've dined at the finest spots worldwide. And those dream rides I used to fantasize about, well, they're parked in my driveway now.

Throughout my journey, I've been blessed with recognition that goes beyond my wildest dreams. It's an honor to share that I've been nominated for numerous awards, a testament to the impact one can have in their community and beyond. Here's a glimpse at some of these accolades:

I've been named Omega Man of the Year by Omega Psi Phi Fraternity Inc., a recognition that holds a special place in my heart. Being named a Rising Leader of Palm Beach County with Nonprofits First of Palm Beach County and Leadership Palm Beach County marked my growing influence in local leadership. My work as a Community Activist didn't go unnoticed either, with an award from the City of Boynton Beach's MLK Committee.

Bethune Cookman University acknowledged me with the 40 Under 40 "Movers and Shakers Award," a nod to my efforts in stirring positive change. The sisters of Zeta Phi Beta Sorority Inc. honored me with the Blue Revue Award, while the South Annual Conference Eleventh Episcopal District AME Church presented me with the Bishop Award for Business & Professional Services.

I was also an honoree at Greater St. Paul AME's 61st Annual Pink Tea. I was named one of Palm Beach County's 100 Most Influential Business Leaders. I received the Superior Service Award from Omega Psi Phi Fraternity Inc. The Inner-City Youth Golfers, Inc. presented me with the Community Giants "Founder's Award," a reflection of my commitment to youth and community development.

Each of these awards is a chapter in my story, a story of dedication, perseverance, and a relentless commitment to making a difference. They are not just accolades but reminders of the responsibility I carry to continue being a beacon of hope and change.

At the heart of everything I am and everything I do are my incredible children – Ricky, Jr., Rickia, and Rickiya. Along with them are my solid-as-a-rock family, the special lady in my life, and businesses that are hitting new highs daily. I've poured love and resources back into my community and church, making sure the blessings cycle back.

Some folks will never understand the work I put in to obtain the results I currently have. I have worked hard for what I have and what I have accomplished. I've carved out a pretty sweet spot for myself in this world, but trust me, this is just the prelude. The best chapters are still unfolding.

Chapter Thirteen Messages for the Next Generation

"Your destiny isn't determined by the limitations others place on you ..."

Before I close this book, let's take a minute to vibe on a future note. We've walked through my journey, step by step, from my gritty beginnings to the mountaintop moments. But now, it's about y'all, the next wave, the upcoming hustlers, the future leaders. This final chapter is my heart and soul poured out, a collection of gems I've picked up along the way.

These are more than words, they're life lessons. Lessons on grinding, on pushing through, on never letting the flame inside of you die. It's my hope that as you read this, you feel the ancestral pull and drive from those who paved the way.

I'll be taking these messages to stages, sharing them with crowds, and sparking fire in the next generation. Let's make sure our stories, our struggles, our triumphs echo through time. It's on us to pass down the torch, to ensure that the next generation rises even higher. So, family, are you ready to be inspired? Let's get to it.

Advice For Those Living in Poverty

Let's talk for a moment. Now, you've heard me speak on the grind and the hustle, but let's dissect the system and structures that keep many of us in the cycle of struggle. You see, sociology teaches us that our environments, our neighborhoods, the schools we attend, and the systems in place — they all play a role in our lives, more than we sometimes want to admit.

Growing up in the grip of poverty isn't just about lack of money, it's the societal barriers, the expectations, and the pre-written narratives that get handed down to us. When society paints a picture of you based on where you come from, your color, or your zip code, it's easy to feel confined to that narrative.

But here's the deal, I'm not saying it's easy, but breaking free from these systemic chains is a combination of mindset, education, and community. Sociology underscores the importance of understanding these structures so we can navigate them. By getting educated, not just in the traditional sense, but understanding the socio-economic dynamics, the political games, and the local resources available, we start arming ourselves.

We must tap into community resources. Network with those who've managed to break free from the chains of poverty. Understand the importance of mentorship, both seeking it and giving back. Remember, each one, teach one.

As we rise, we gotta lift our brothers and sisters. It's about creating generational knowledge, not just generational wealth.

No cap, the journey is tough. But understanding the societal forces at play, and more importantly, how to work within and against them, is crucial. It's like playing chess, but instead of pawns and kings, we're working with opportunities and setbacks. With the right moves, strategies, and a community that's got your back, you can navigate out of any struggle. Stay woke, stay resilient, and always stay hungry for knowledge because knowledge is power, but only when you use it. And with power, we can reshape the narratives handed to us.

Advice to those in the System

Another piece of advice I want to share hits close to home. I know firsthand that for many of us, life's journey sometimes has detours that lead us to the Criminal Justice System.

Now, let me tell you, re-entering the world after doing time isn't just walking out the gates to freedom. It's about navigating a whole new maze of obstacles, judgments, and labels that society's ready to slap on you.

When you have a criminal record, every door might feel like it's closing in your face—jobs, housing, even reconnecting with some family or friends. But here's the real, just because the system's been designed one way, doesn't mean we can't find our own blueprint for success.

First thing, own your story. Don't let it be something that's whispered about you, you tell it. Let people know that you made mistakes, but those mistakes don't define you. They're just chapters in your book, not the whole story.

Education and skill development are non-negotiable. There are community programs and organizations designed to help folks reintegrate into society. These programs provide job training, counseling, and resources. Look into these programs and organizations. Equip yourself with marketable tools and skills that make you indispensable. Remember, you're not just competing, you're demonstrating that your past doesn't determine your future potential.

Rebuilding trust is going to take time. Start with your family, friends, and community. Even if it's one person at a time, those relationships are your foundation. And once again, I stress seeking mentorship. Mentorship is gold. So, find someone who's been through it, who's navigated those treacherous waters and came out on top. Their guidance and their lessons are invaluable.

Of course, I emphasize the value of networking. Yeah, I know, that sounds all corporate, but I'm talking about genuine connections. Build relationships with people who believe in second chances, who can vouch for your character and work ethic.

Lastly, don't just reintegrate, *redefine.* Use your experiences, your lessons, and your story to uplift and educate. Maybe that's mentoring the youth, starting a support group, or even advocating for policy changes. Be that beacon of hope for others in similar shoes.

We're not ignoring the fact that society's got its biases. But we're also not letting that be the end of our story. Your past is just that, the past! Your future is a blank slate, waiting for you to etch your legacy. Hold your head high, walk with purpose, and remember you aren't just surviving, you're thriving.

Advice To Young Fathers

Another thought I would like to leave with you is about the greatest role you will experience as a man and that is fatherhood. Now imagine stepping into those shoes while you're still growing up yourself. Visualize becoming a dad as a teenager. Man, it's like being thrown in the deep end when you're still learning to swim. But listen up because I've got some wisdom to lay on you.

First things first, own it. It is not how young you are, but how mature you choose to be. The child is looking up to you and needs you, whether you're 16 or 60. Age might define your youth, but responsibility defines your manhood. Don't let pride, fear, or immaturity get in the way of you stepping up.

Don't feel pressured to act like you've got it all figured out. No one is expecting you to have it all figured out. Seek wisdom from the OGs—your dad, uncles, mentors, older brothers, people who've walked the path and got stories and lessons to share. They've got a playbook so tap into it.

Education is paramount, young kings. Just because you're a father, doesn't mean your dreams get benched. Stay in school, keep pushing forward. Your education is not just about you anymore, it's a ladder for your little one's future as well.

Your circle is more crucial now than ever. Surround yourself with folks who uplift, who challenge, who support. And those who drain or distract, it may be time to reassess and recalibrate those relationships.

Bond with your child. Don't get it twisted, you can and should be fun and playful with your child. The sound of your laughter, the warmth of your hugs—those things are as nurturing as it gets.

To the mothers out there, I urge you to respect and support the fathers of your children. Regardless of where you all stand romantically, communication is vital. Co-parenting requires teamwork. Yeah, there'll be disagreements, but remember, it's about what's best for the child, not winning an argument.

Lastly, remember to take care of yourself, mentally, physically, and emotionally. Remember, you can't pour from an empty cup. Reflect, grow, and evolve. You'll make mistakes, but let each one be a lesson, not a regret.

Being a young father isn't about what you've lost, it's about what you've gained. A chance to mold a life, to leave a legacy, to rise and show the world that age is but a number when it comes to love, sacrifice, and dedication. Embrace fatherhood. Own it and walk the path with your head held high. You got this, young king.

Advice to Entrepreneurs

If there's one thing I've learned on this wild ride called life, it's that taking that leap into entrepreneurship is not for the faint of heart. But if you're looking to carve out your empire and secure the bag the *Petty Way*, I've got some gems to drop on you.

First off, don't just chase the paper, chase the passion. The most successful businesses aren't built on dollar signs alone. They're built on fire, love, and an unwavering drive. Find what lights you up, what keeps you grinding even when the nights get long, and lead with that energy.

Next, knowledge is your sharpest tool in the shed. Invest in it. Read books, attend seminars, get mentors, join mastermind groups. The game is always evolving, and the real hustlers never stop learning.

Now don't get it twisted, entrepreneurship is a marathon, not a sprint. Pace yourself. Building wealth isn't about quick cash, it's about long-term investments, sustainable growth, and financial freedom.

Consider creating multiple streams of income, not just one hustle. The ultimate goal should be to earn, save, and invest your money so it will work for you while you are sleeping good at night.

Remember, your network is your net worth. Increase your social capital by building genuine relationships, not just the "Hey, what can you do for me?" relationships. You need to build the real, "How can we elevate each other?" connections.

Every handshake, every conversation can be a step closer to your next opportunity.

Now, let's talk mindset because mindset is everything. Prepare and expect setbacks but see them as setups for comebacks. Think with the end in mind. This will allow you to see the vision clearly. Create the plan and work the plan to ensure that your vision and dreams come true. Entrepreneurship will test you, break you, rebuild you, but always keep your vision clear. Where your mind goes, your energy flows. Stay focused on your goals and the reasons why you started.

Protect your brand like it's your baby. Your reputation, your work ethic, your integrity, they all play into how folks perceive your brand. Show up consistently, authentically, and always overdeliver.

As you rise and the coins start stacking and success starts rolling in, don't forget your roots. Give back. Whether it's mentoring the next generation, supporting local causes, or investing back into the community, keep the circle of blessings moving.

At the end of the day, accumulating wealth the Petty Way is about more than just dollar signs. It's about legacy. It's about building something that stands the test of time, that inspires others and makes a mark. So go forth, future moguls, and light up the path with your greatness. The world ain't seen nothing yet.

<u>**Advice On living in your purpose**</u>

Stepping back and peeping the scene of life, there's this undeniable truth I've grasped: living with purpose, in peace, and embracing health is the realest kind of wealth. Let me break it down for you.

Living life with purpose isn't about what society says you should be doing; it's about tuning into your own frequency and catching the rhythm that resonates with your soul. Ask yourself, what sets your heart on fire. What would you do if time and money weren't factors? That's your purpose speaking. Don't muffle its voice. Honor it, chase it, embrace it. At the end of the day, a life filled with purpose is one where regrets don't find space.

Now, let's rap about peace. Inner peace is like that silent anchor in a chaotic storm that keeps you grounded. It's understanding that life will throw curveballs, and not all battles are yours to fight. Sometimes the most profound statement you can make is to remain silent, to take a step back and let things be.

Your peace, your sanctuary, is sacred. Guard it. It's about setting boundaries, knowing when to say no, and recognizing that your mental and emotional well-being comes before any kind of drama or negativity.

Speaking of well-being, let's not sleep on the importance of health. The body you're in is the only one you're gonna get, so nourish it, cherish it, move it, and groove with it. Exercise is about more than looking good, it's about feeling good, as well.

It's the adrenaline, the natural high, and the mental clarity that you get from exercising. And don't get me started on what you feed your body.

Good food is more than just flavor, it's fuel for the body. The brighter, fresher, and less processed, the better. But remember, balance is key. Treat yourself every now and then. Life's too short not to savor the sweetness.

In essence, living on purpose, in peace, and healthy is about understanding your worth. It's about respecting the journey, embracing the lessons, and always striving for growth. So, step out, head held high, and create the melody that'll become the soundtrack of your life. The world is waiting for your unique rhythm, so make it count.

Throughout the pages of my journey, from the sun-soaked lanes of Florida to the bustling business streets, I've laid bare the essence of life's ever-winding path. From the harsh bite of poverty to the elation of enterprise success, my story stands as a testament to the enduring spirit of human resilience. Living beyond petty isn't just a phrase to me, it encapsulates my transformation, a journey from life's most challenging moments to its soaring heights.

As we close this chapter, I want these tales of struggle and success, love and loss, dreams, and realities, to serve not just as an inspiration but as a clarion call.

To the next generation reading this, I encourage you to chart your own path, blaze your own trail, and always remember, the essence of life lies not just in the destination but in the journey itself. Embrace every twist and turn, for within the journey lies the essence of a story worth telling. Beyond the confines of these pages, may you too find your life Beyond Petty.

<u>Advice on Healthy Relationships</u>

Listen closely, because what I'm about to share with you is the culmination of years of experiences, trials, and profound love. When it comes to building a healthy romantic relationship, it's not just about the fire of passion but also about the steadiness of companionship.

First and foremost, understand that love is not just an emotion—it's an action. It's the little things you do daily, the sacrifices you make, the understanding you exhibit, and the patience you muster. Love is choosing the same person over and over again, even when times are tough. Especially when times are tough.

First you must remember that communication is your lifeline. Many relationships have gone astray due to assumptions, misunderstandings, and unsaid words. Talk to each other. Even more importantly, listen. Listen not just while you're waiting to respond but listen to understand. And when you're wrong? Admit it. When you're hurt, express it. When you're in love, celebrate it!

Respect cannot be overstated. It's the bedrock upon which all relationships stand. Value your partner's feelings, dreams, and boundaries. Their aspirations and fears are as valid as yours. In moments of conflict, approach the situation with an aim to resolve, not to win. In love, when one loses, both lose.

Intimacy also plays a crucial role. And no, I'm not just talking about physical intimacy, although that too is essential. Emotional intimacy—being vulnerable, sharing your deepest hopes, dreams, fears, and insecurities, that's the glue that binds hearts together. Create a safe space for each other where vulnerabilities can be shared without judgment.

Lastly, never stop courting your partner. The chase shouldn't end once you're together. Continue to discover new things about each other. Go on dates, surprise each other, keep the spark alive. But remember, it's the everyday moments—the laughter over a shared joke, the silent comfort in holding hands, the shared glance across a crowded room that truly makes a love story.

Times are different now; the world is ever evolving. But the foundation of love remains unchanged. Value, respect, trust, communication, and commitment are timeless.

To the next generation, I hope you cherish these truths and build relationships that are enduring, enriching, and, above all, filled with boundless love.

As I turn the page on this chapter of my life, I can't help but reflect on the many twists, turns, and lessons that have defined my journey. Each chapter of this book, and indeed, each chapter of my life, has been an intimate exploration of growth, resilience, adversity, and triumph. From the backstreets of my youth to the boardrooms of adulthood, the stories etched in these pages are more than mere recollections—they're the very essence of who I've become.

Growing up, the stark reality of racial disparities, economic challenges, and societal expectations tried to box me in. But with every challenge came invaluable lessons. The lessons of determination from my early years, the understanding of community and its indomitable spirit, the profound importance of family ties, and the discovery of my own voice amid the clamor. The stories of love, of loss, of battles fought both outside and within, and the relentless pursuit of purpose and identity have all intertwined to shape my worldview.

To those who read my journey, understand that life will hand you complexities that sometimes feel insurmountable. It might attempt to define you, confine you, even malign you. But it's crucial to remember that your response to life's challenges is where your true power lies. Your ability to rise, adapt, learn, and push forward is what defines you.

It's easy to get bogged down by life's pettiness, but your destiny isn't determined by the limitations others place on you—it's crafted by your spirit, your resilience, and the legacy you wish to leave behind.

As for the future, I remain ever hopeful. Hopeful that the generations that come after me will draw strength from my tales, see the humanity behind every statistic, and recognize the power of perseverance. Hopeful that my children, and their children, will live in a world where they are judged not by the color of their skin but by the content of their character. And hopeful that every person, irrespective of their background, will see that they too can overcome, evolve, and transcend their circumstances.

In the end, life is far too short and far too precious to get caught up in the smallness of things. The lessons I've learned, the struggles I've faced, and the victories I've celebrated have all taught me the importance of looking at the bigger picture, of moving forward with purpose, passion, and positivity. I urge you to do the same. Rise above, look beyond, and live a life that is, in every sense, beyond petty.

"Mr. Wonderful"

To contact Ricky:

web: BeyondPetty.com **email:** info@beyondpetty.com